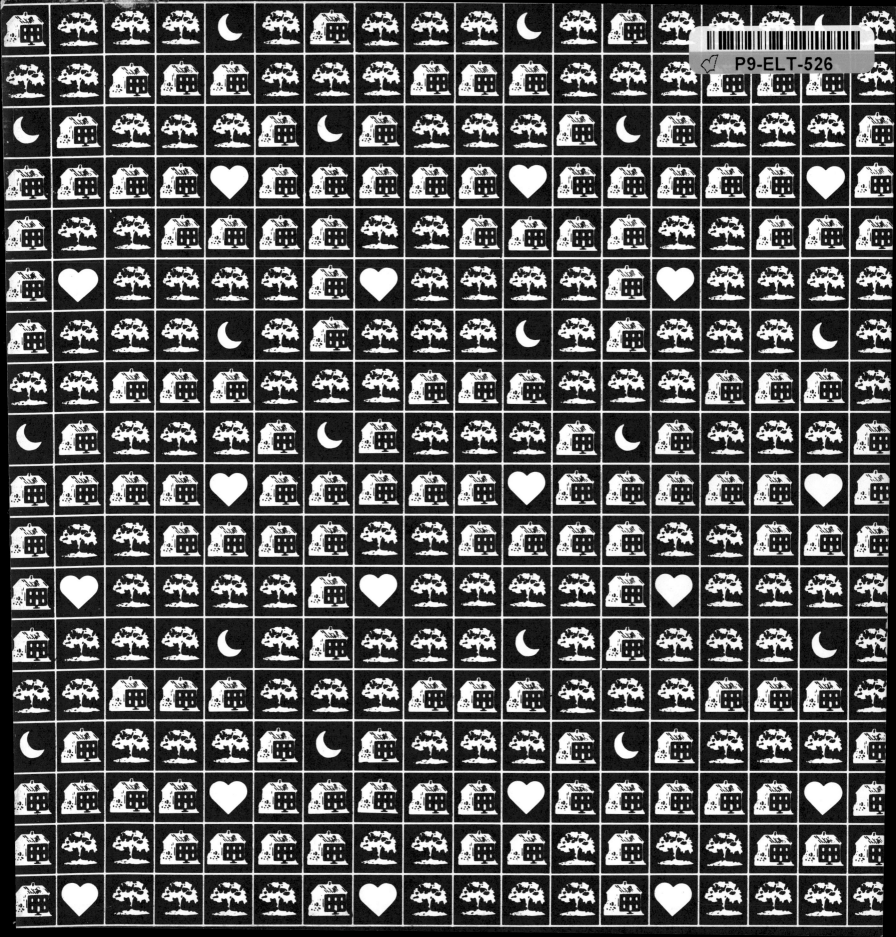

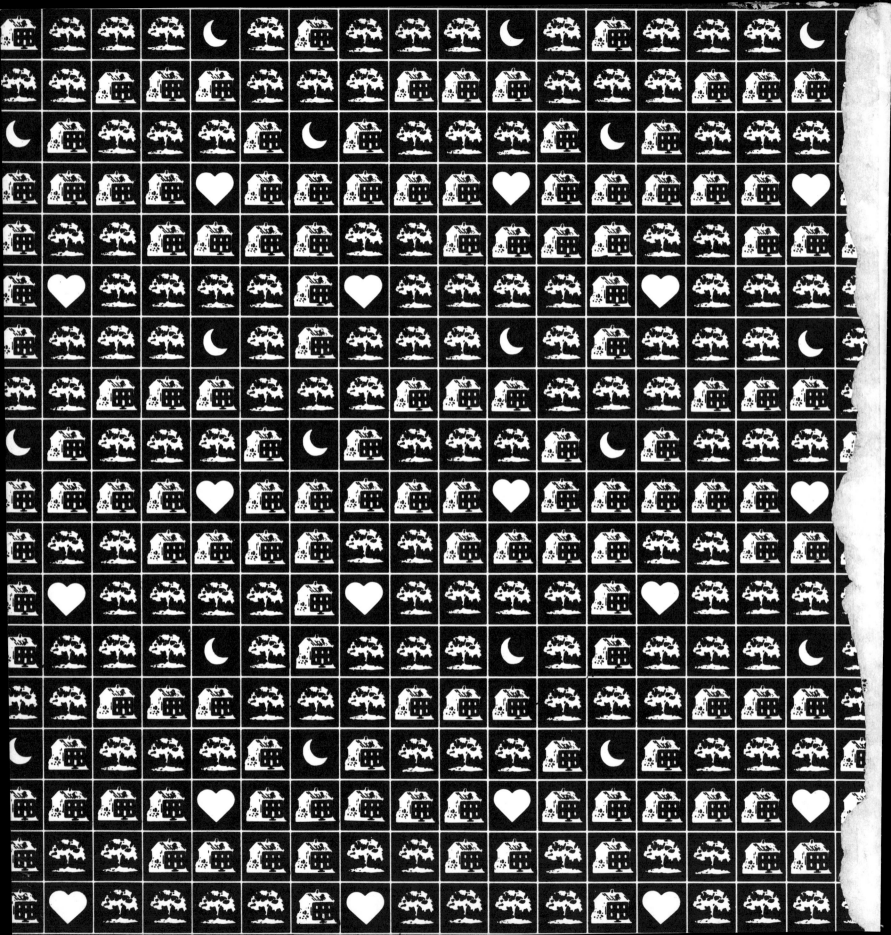

NEW COUNTRY GEAR®

AMERICAN V·I·E·W

COLOR YOUR HOME BEAUTIFUL
WITH COUNTRY COLORS, PATTERNS AND FORMS

BY RAYMOND WAITES
BETTYE MARTIN
AND NORMA SKURKA
FOOD BY MAXIME DE LA FALAISE

DESIGN BY RAYMOND WAITES
DESIGN ASSOCIATE: JANICE WARNER

1817
HARPER & ROW, PUBLISHERS, New York
Cambridge, Philadelphia, San Francisco, London, Mexico City, São Paulo, Sydney

In memory of Tom Meloy, who believed in the impossible dream.

Carl Ally and Emil Garganno, who provided a home for Gear its first year.

John Jamison, who guided us through our first year of financial planning as a friend and not as a client of Goldman-Sachs.

Claudia Koeze, my daughter, whose independent spirit and understanding made possible my career.

Doris Stone and Olla Binford, the home support team that gave me peace of mind and encouragement.

Max Block, Jr. and Walter Marple, our attorneys.

Jim Lang of the Economic Development Association.

Beatrice Appleyard Waites, my mother, who instilled in me the belief that I could tackle any task and always do my best.

Nancy Waites, my wife, who has grown with me since we met, who has brought so many beautiful family heirlooms into our lives, and who has supported the free-dom and risk-taking

needed to make ideas become reality.

Maltby Sykes and Marrietta Kettunen, my university professors at Auburn who opened the first design doors.

Ben Thompson, founder of Design Research, who changed the American retail store.

The late Armi Ratia and Ristomatti Ratia, my mentors and owners of Marimekko.

Michael Haskins, who pops in and out of my life, helping start so many projects.

Suzy Tuck Griffin and Joe Meyers, our on-site people for the Gear Barn.

Michael Greenberg, friend, who gave me the first quilt swatches that started my love for country fabrics.

Tom McCavera, photographer and loyal supporter of Gear.

Lilo Raymond and Michael Skott, photographers.

TO WILLIAM MUSHAM: WITHOUT BILL ALL THIS WOULD NOT BE POSSIBLE

The Gear Board of Directors: Neele Stearns, Jr., Lee Hall, Jud Lober.

Meg Groves, our first employee at Gear, and to everyone who has contributed to Gear over the last six years: Doree Albritton, Monica Barnwell, Susan Baum, Nancy Blanchard, Katrina Blumenstock, James Bogan, Jane Bogart, Suzanne Bonne, Doris Broadley, Jim Byler, Irene Calvo, Jaclynn Carroll, Alison Choate, Craig Cook, Sarah Cooke, Phyllis Cox, Deborah Dassaro, Michelle Desveaux, Stephen Earle, David Ehrenreich, James Finkle, Lynn Fischer, Connie Formby, Peggy Gardner, Nancy Green, Oshiel Hand, Barbara Hanson, Brenda Hanson, Ellen Harewood, Sarah Hartman, Kathleen Hartney, Steve Haws, Jane Hertzmark, Barbara Herzfeld, Cynthia Huffling, Anne Jaroszewicz, Andrea Jessup, Lisette Jimenez, Edward Kaeding, Kelley Kapfer, Klaudia Khasina, Akira Kimura, Michael Kirkpatrick, Margaret Layton, Jenny Lee, Cheryl Lewin, Katherine Longely, Patty Lowry, Margaret Milley, Janice Mitchell, Robert Mojica, Jeffrey Morris, Frances Nannery, Bob Novak, Amy O'Shea, LeAnn Pegram, Nina Pelle-grini, Eva Pietrzak, Joan Polisano, Joyce Post, Janet Racy, John Rapp, Jean Rich, Andrea Rosenblum, Howard Rzeszewski, Margaret Sabo, Judith Sacks, Claudia Sandoval, Nohra Sandoval, Jenny Sandoval, Jane Schwacke, Amy Sherwood, Florrie Shore, Penny Sikalis, Sarita Silvers, Ann Snow, Peggy Snyder, Dorothea Suino, Susanne Thierry, Karen Vati, Linda Velez, Bob Weisell, Claudia Wielandt, Heather Wielandt, Amy Wrapp.

Our industry friends: Marc Balmuth, Peter Strawbridge, Carl Levine, Bill and Gene Rappaport, Marty Bristow, Bob McCabe, Lee Gunst, Asher Berlan, Bill Snyder, Don Graeber, JoAnn Barwick.

In memory of Bruce Benepe, our first licensee, who believed and supported us.

Our manufacturers: Wallcoverings by Imperial, Fabrics by Cohama Riverdale, Sheets and Towels by Springs Industries, Kitchen Textiles by Kitchen Gear, Gear Bags by Players USA, Fabrics by Covington, Homesewing Patterns by Butterick, Baskets by American Bravo, Paperware by Contempo, Crib Ensembles by Dundee Mills, Nursery Furniture by ChildCraft, Car Seats/Playards by Century Products, Stationery by C.R. Gibson, Dinnerware by Hartstone, Bath Gear by Jakson, Blankets by The Three Weavers, Woodenware by MaLeck, Closet Gear by Ashland, Infant Clothing by The Schwab Company, Housewares by General Housewares.

For further information on the above licensees, contact Gear Inc., 19 West 34th Street, New York, N.Y. 10001, (212) 736-8499.

And, to all people throughout this country who have contributed to the American Design Movement in their own way.

Ripe for Preservation

Truly American, this house is a mixture of whimsy and function. Although sadly neglected, it is salvageable. The straight roofline indicates that the rafters and roof are still strong. Stranded by the side of a highway, this house is probably doomed. And, yet, such houses can often still be bought for under $15,000. What a loss: a relic of the farm life that reared generations of Americans.

HOUSE FOR SAVING

Peter Neumann/Stock Market

PORCH SALE
This dilapidated farmhouse is begging to be saved.

AMERICAN

A FOCUS ON OUR AMERICAN VISUAL VOCABULARY: THE COLORS,

This is a totally different kind of design book. In it, we show the origins of American design, the elements from which it grew. But, more importantly, we focus on the colors, patterns, and forms that are still all around us. Each of us retains built-in images and impressions of the towns and countryside that reared us. Those impressions form our American visual vocabulary, and they are deep in our psyche. One needn't travel far from the cities to encounter the artifacts of our living heritage: a barn emblazoned with hearts on its roof, houses smiling with gingerbread trim, window shutters with playful cutouts of arrows and moons. Instinctively, we love America's exuberant spirit.

American design, we believe, is the product of two distinct influences. The first influence is that of tradition—of the elements and artifacts of our cultural history: folk art and country objects made by our ancestors, such as quilts, homespun fabrics, redware pottery, salt-glaze crocks, duck decoys, dollhouses, hooked rugs, and twig furniture. These simple objects of everyday life have been raised today to the level of art. They contribute the unique charm and whimsy of American design. The second influence, equally strong, is present-day technology. Americans are "doers." We have always embraced the new in industrial and scientific advances, in mechanization and electronics. We naturally tinker and invent, react and change, adapt and improve. These two distinct but powerful native forces blend into today's design and we call it American Artech. It is design that is both comfortable and innovative.

So much contributed to our national character. No single culture can be said to have formed this pioneering nation. The heritage of the English along the Eastern Seaboard has to be balanced against the Spanish

ARTECH

THE PATTERNS, AND THE FORMS THAT ARE ALL AROUND US.

colonization on the opposite coast. And while the French, Dutch, and Spanish were carving out enclaves on the nation's shores, an ancient Indian civilization was flourishing in the interior. In the arid Southwest, their building techniques are still used in the adobe construction of New Mexico and Arizona. America continued to take in pioneers and our new immigrants from every land enrich our culture with their own ethnic heritage. From this marvelous polyglot of sources emerged the American visual vocabulary.

By the middle of the last century we had entered the machine age. Railroads linked the urban centers with rural towns; electricity reached out to the farthest outposts by the Rural Electrification Program of 1935; automobiles brought freedom of movement; the airplane gave instant access to any part of the world; television opened up ideas and social interchange on a global scale. Finally, and most signifi-

cantly, space science planted a man on the moon and changed for all time our planetary conceit. Our earth, viewed from the moon, appeared exceedingly fragile and vulnerable. These technological advances changed our view of the world—they brought us closer to each other and to other cultures.

In the light of 20th-century developments, the values that built this nation seem all the more precious. What we sense in the humble arts of our ancestors is a spirit that is America.

Through these pages, we want you to learn to appreciate our visual and adaptive heritage and to use it as a foundation for your daily life. The rich varieties of American architecture and design are not merely historic footnotes but springboards for innovation and adaptation into our own contemporary environments. This is a book of pictures you can read.

This is a very personal book, too. We

want to tell you about the simple process of seeing and about how design happens. We hope to break down the mystique and mystery that surround design so that you, too, can be your own designer.

When we began this book, we sat down and talked amongst ourselves about how we did things, such as pull a room together, or create the New Country Gear line of wallpaper, fabrics, and other products for the home. Through this discussion, we realized that design for us is not an intellectual process, but rather represents an emotional response to color, to form, to shape, and most of all to the familiar things that are all around us. Not surprisingly, we discovered that we were greatly influenced by the things we knew and loved best: objects that jumped out at us in an antique shop, colors we kept putting into our wardrobes, family memorabilia, seashells picked up on the beach, a plate we bought on vacation, a party someone gave us, an impromptu evening with friends. These are small things all, but when added up, they constitute a lifetime of special moments and memories.

Color, we realized, is integral to the design process. Color can create a mood of excitement or calm. It can bind many other-wise unrelated objects and patterns together. It is because color underlies the whole process of design, showing the links and relationships among pattern, texture, and form, that we chose to divide the chapters in this book by color.

We also discovered that it isn't necessary to spend a lot of money to design with wonderful, personal style. Some of the things we loved most were taken from the meadows and fields, things that other people might even throw away. Design, it turned out, is getting to know ourselves, and to feel confident enough to say: "This is something I really love and want to live with" or "This is the color I'm really happy about." These simple, universal responses, became the blueprint according to which we made most of our decorating decisions.

Finally, this book is not only about the colors, patterns, and forms of our visual vocabulary; it's about an attitude and a way of thinking. Design is not just about rooms but about how we relate to them. It's a way of looking at the simplest things, at the moments of our daily lives, and finding something special in them. A home is made up of a million moments—the fragrance of a flower bouquet, the flickering light of candles, the spicy taste of a bowl of chili, the smell of a pie baking in the oven, the crisp feel of a cotton napkin, the coolness of marble or glass, the smell of fresh pine branches at Christmas.

Life is a mosaic of these simple moments. Bringing them all together is the fun part of making a home. Each day should be a joy. When we begin to think about living in our homes this way, it removes the terror that is so often a part of design. We can be overwhelmed by the big plan, that is, by all the many decorating decisions that go into planning a home. We can become afraid to tackle it. But we can all start small, working on each detail, one moment at a time. Work toward making each moment beautiful: setting the table, making the bed a certain way, creating a bouquet of flowers or even vegetables, massed in a big basket, or slipcovering the sofa.

When we began this book, we were surprised that so many people shared our American view. We are only one voice—there are many others across the nation. They constitute a movement of people who appreciate the casual, relaxed way of living. Many people love and use the objects of our country heritage. A great part of making this book was learning from others.

And just as we learned from people who embraced our attitudes, so we wanted to share our thoughts and knowledge with you. Throughout this book, we speak about editing the details of our personal lives. AMERICAN VIEW is our way of editing. You may respond to the historical side of American design or you may prefer the innovative, modern side. Only you can decide how much or how little works for you.

It was also our goal to speak directly to you. This is why we set up the book as a series of interviews so that the people whose homes appear here share their thoughts with you. We have created a design dialogue, and hope that in this way we have made design much more friendly and accessible. Our ideas are available to everybody. Our designs often develop by trial and error, and we share that process with you in this book.

It would be our greatest joy if all who read this book were changed by it. We'd love you to say "I can do it." Look around you, learn to appreciate what you see there and to use it. That's the process—and it still works. This book is the product of people, and, in the process of creating it, we've had fun. We hope that our joy comes through to you.

Raymond Waites, Bettye Martin, Norma Skurka

Village Green

This enchanting cottage has stood on the side of the village green in East Hampton, Long Island since the end of the 17th century. Robert Dayton, a farmer and fisherman, built it around 1680. It was in ruins in 1907 when restoration by the Gustav Bueks of Brooklyn began. Today, Home Sweet Home is owned by the village of East Hampton and is open to the public.

Raymond Waites

HOME SWEET HOME

1680's SALTBOX
It was about this historic house that the song "Home Sweet Home" was written.

Multiple Use

Barns served as stable, feed and grain bin, storage space, and garage. The exceptionally tall doors allowed a horse-drawn cart to travel through the barn without the rider having to dismount.

Colonial High-Tech

Barns are the workhorses of indigenous American architecture and are so easily converted into modern homes.

CEDAR SHAKE BARN

AZALEA HOUSE

Burst of Color

Azaleas echo the burst of color of the flaming pink roof shingles on this cottage. Color sequences like this are constantly greeting us as we travel through America. This confident owner (and gardener) obviously loved pink and planted the azaleas to provide this visual connection in celebration of spring color.

TOWN HOUSE

Barry O'Rourke/Stock Market

Historic Color

A historic house in Providence, R.I., decorates the street scene with its blaze of yellow clapboards. The black shutters and windows outlined in white balance the yellow's brilliance. The house radiates warmth and sunny exuberance. It shows that its owner had the sure hand to use color in bold strokes.

Barn in the Northwest

This aged barn in the far northwest is a soft rusty red, the result of years of weathering to this rich patina.

Windmill fragment is a piece of industrial art.

Painted tin roof is
scarred by weather to
a glowing russet.

YELLOW SURPRISE

Sun-baked in Snow

As New England is a region of white clapboard buildings, the West is an area of sun-baked clay and adobe. Trees for building are less prevalent than the pervasive clay, which has been the dominant building material since ancient times.

Lisl Dennis

Adobes in shades of rose take their colors from native clays.

PUEBLO TEXTURES

Raymond Waites

Pueblo Architecture

The Pueblo Indian dwellings dating from the eleventh century in New Mexico are often a shock to visitors whose knowledge of this ancient culture is scant. Pueblo housing was notched into the sheer rock cliffs facing a valley and low-lying stream. Densely populated, the dwellings in this village extend for a mile across the valley and were seven to ten stories high, the rooms reached by slender wood ladders. It was a sophisticated and complex culture that, even in its abandoned state, presents an image of mysterious beauty. The color and textural interplay makes this a stunning artifact. This was a human example of small-town living in pre-Columbian America.

Get It Right

The mortar has to be very carefully mixed for color and consistency. If it's too hard, it can crack the stone when it expands in extremes of weather. The original mortar was a sort of mauve-beige (the dirt here is actually purple in color). I found that a weak mix of mortar, white lime, local clay and sand comes out right.

Ken chips away at the plaster to restore the original stone walls.

Carole Le Van

RESTORING A STONE HOUSE

Ken Le Van, industrial designer, and Carole Le Van, weaver: We bought this Pennsylvania stone farmhouse three years ago and have been restoring it ever since. It was in the same family for ten generations and my own family has been in Pennsylvania for ten generations so I feel very close to it. It was built by a German family in the 1800's but it is English Quaker in architectural style. Around 1830, an addition was made and the stonework of the newer section isn't nearly as fine as the original work. Some time later, in the Greek Revival period when it became fashionable to live in a white house, many owners plastered over their stone houses and that's probably what happened to this one. I'm removing the plaster and it's a monumental job. But once you begin, you're stuck and have to go on!

Keep at It

I can only work an eight-foot-square section per day. I bang away with a hammer and chisel until the mortar chips and then I pry it off. When I'm lucky, it comes off in big chunks but more often it just flakes. For the hard-to-reach places, I use a little air hammer I bought at an auto shop. Believe it or not, this is the easy part. The hard part is repointing the stone and getting the mortar to look like the original.

Keep a Porch

The porch is a Victorian addition but we've kept it on because it looks like it belongs.

Peter Wentz Historic Farmstead

This stone farmstead, c. 1758, looks as modern as anything built today. The walls of red sandstone, quarried down the road in Worcester, Pa., are a graphic counterpoint to the regularity of the hand-shaved roof shingles. The mullioned windows and doors are another surprise. Black frames outlining the white windows set up a modern grid pattern that contrasts with the busy texture of the stone. This play of dark against light, grid against random pattern, is the source for many contemporary designs and patterns.

Black frames around white mullioned windows is a grid pattern against the textured stone.

Visit a Museum

The Peter Wentz Farmstead (where George Washington headquartered in 1777) is a museum today, thirty-five miles from Philadelphia, at the crossing of Routes 73 and 363 in Worcester. It's well worth a visit.

STONE FARMSTEAD

Michael Skott

Trellised silo is a screened patio.

Lattice grid covers the end wall, an unexpected pattern for the exterior.

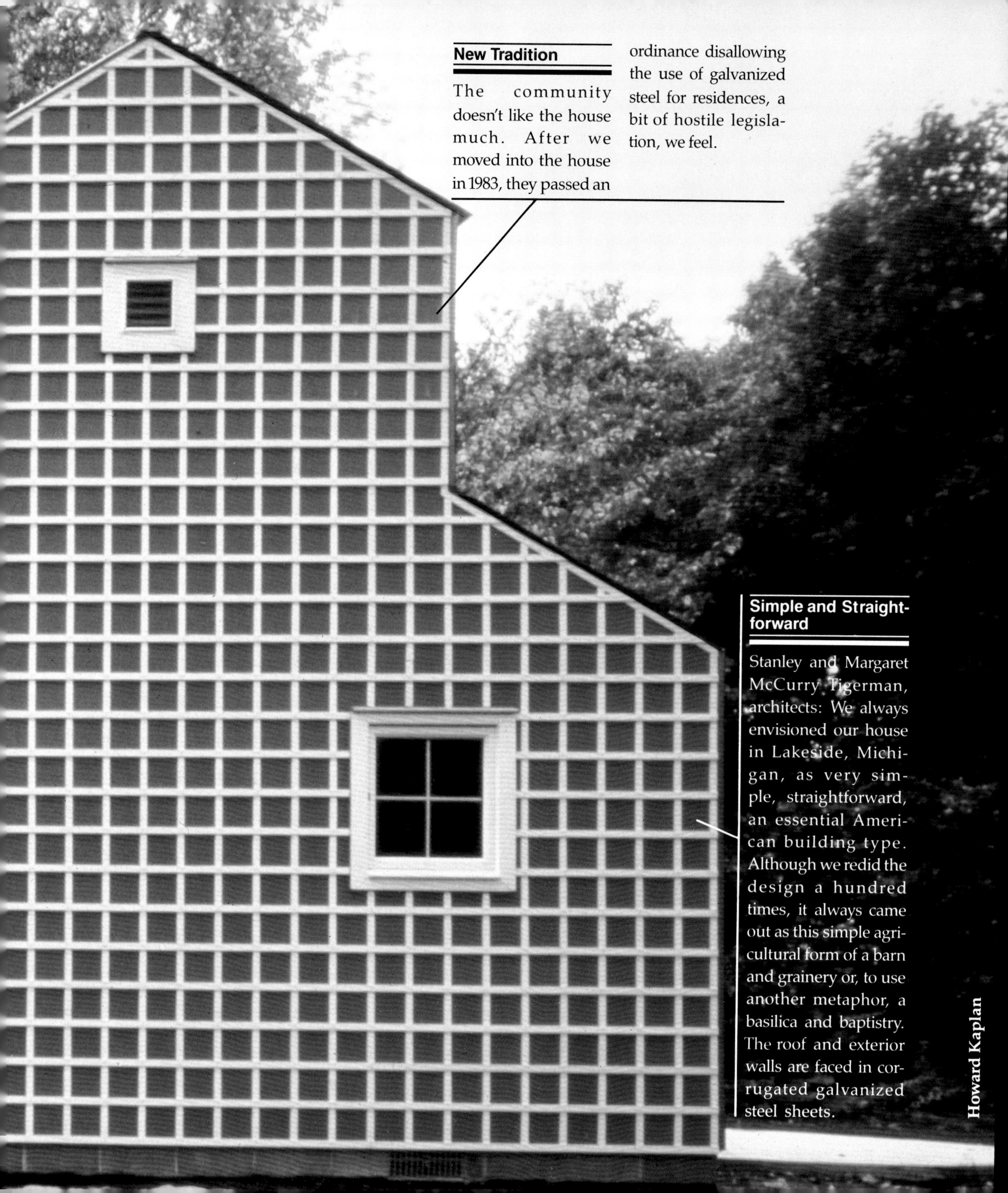

New Tradition

The community doesn't like the house much. After we moved into the house in 1983, they passed an ordinance disallowing the use of galvanized steel for residences, a bit of hostile legislation, we feel.

Simple and Straightforward

Stanley and Margaret McCurry Tigerman, architects: We always envisioned our house in Lakeside, Michigan, as very simple, straightforward, an essential American building type. Although we redid the design a hundred times, it always came out as this simple agricultural form of a barn and grainery or, to use another metaphor, a basilica and baptistry. The roof and exterior walls are faced in corrugated galvanized steel sheets.

Howard Kaplan

Quaker Notes

Members of the Society of Friends were called Quakers because George Fox, the Englishman who founded the sect in 1650, bade them to "tremble at the word of the Lord." They have no ordained clergy and no liturgy, and their meetinghouses are made as simple as possible. In the life of these early colonists, the public meetinghouse was the social center.

Friends Meetinghouse

The harsh, disciplined life of the settlers is clearly expressed in the austerity of this exquisite meeting-house built in 1787 in Vermont. Its simple peaked roof, repeated in miniature in the side extension, the regularity of the windows, and the unadorned facade give the building an awesome power and spirituality. This is one of the finest examples of Colonial architecture.

Lilo Raymond

18th Century Illusion

Norma: This house in Southwestern Pennsylvania is a graphic expression of American Artech. Viewed from the front, it shares the same spirit as the local farmhouses dating from the 18th century, even to the way they were added onto as the family's needs grew. The façade consists of seven pavilions, each one smaller than the preceding one. They look as though they could be telescoped into one another. In profile, however, the design breaks dramatically into the 21st century. The pitched-roof house shape is completely sheathed in reflective glass, a startling use of a modernday industrial material within this conventional outline. Architect Hugh Newell Jacobsen of Washington, D.C., played with two aesthetics in this fascinating building: historical allusion and visual illusion.

21st Century Technology

While this house appears unconventional and almost playful, it nonetheless grew out of serious functional considerations. The glass wall is a source of solar heat in winter. It faces south so that the sun's rays coming through the glass heat the interiors significantly. In summer, shutters block the sun's entry, relieving the air conditioning load.

Evelyn Hofer

The long pennants are pure ornament. We wanted to see some color and drama on high.

The modern house is consistent with old Block Island architecture of shingle siding and gables.

Make it Affordable

Building the house by hand was a fantastic experience, but I'd never do it again. I'm past forty and I don't have that kind of energy any more. But it was the only way we could afford the house —it cost less than $50,000.

Raymond Waites

Doors are silent pronouncements. They tell us both about the style and architecture of a building and about the people who live there. Doors were always subject to shifts in taste and fashion, much more so than windows or even the house shape. When a new style of architecture came along, it was first manifested in the front door.

The front door of a house is usually meant to impress, and the builders of stately homes lavish attention on it. It proclaims the importance of the house, and thus, of the family who lives there. Through the ages, front doors have been adorned with details of classical architecture; they have been flanked by columns, pillars, and pilasters, inset

Everybody's Doorway

Overhead and side lights, and the red door give this doorway a friendly spirit that we find in houses across the country.

Light Entry

Early houses of the Eastern Seaboard would often have "lights" or windows above the door in order to bring light into the hallway.

RAYMOND WAITES

LILO RAYMOND

38

Mystery Cove

Hewn into the side of a cliff, a magical opening seems to lead deep into the earth. This is one of the earliest forms of housing in America, the cliff dwellings of the Pueblo Indians.

with windows, topped by pediments, friezes, and dentils.

There are, of course, different kinds of doors to suit different purposes. So, impressive as the front door might be, others are designed to be unobtrusive or almost invisible. Back doors, for example, are usually plain and ordinary. They greet us like old friends, lead us into familiar territory.

Blue Moons

Shutters, painted a bright blue, have amusing cutouts shaped like moons. Such playful touches are found on many American houses.

oorways also exhibit strong regional and ethnic differences. Those in New England look completely different from their counterparts in New Orleans or in the Far West. These differences reflect more than the varying styles that characterize each region. They express the aspirations of those who settled in that part of the country and who brought the tastes of their native lands across the ocean. Such regional variations in doorways lend vitality to the street scene. They make walking tours in a strange city so full of surprise.

The closed door gives a clue to who and what resides within; it is the outer limit of someone else's private world. Beyond the closed door is a special world—to enter is to venture into another's territory. A closed door to a

Windmill Door

This doorway to a windmill on the eastern shore of Long Island has been weathered by the salt air. The door is made of a row of planks held together on the inside with wood braces.

Log Cabin

The flapping of the screen door against the frame was a familiar sound to scores of Americans who fled to country cottages in summer.

RAYMOND WAITES

MICHAEL SKOTT

place we've never been signals excitement. There is a sense of expectation, like being handed a wrapped present. What's inside? Often, the first glimpse into a new space is the occasion for a silent thrill. But first one must traverse that portal to a place that is new and unknown. That's the reason why we are drawn to those doors that give a sense of welcome, either by color, hardware, or with a wreath or garland.

Wood and Stucco

Compare this blocky, rustic door in New Mexico to the doorway pictured beside it to see how far the decoration of the American door has come.

Full of Fancy

At the turn of the century, it was considered ideal to live in a fanciful cottage with a trellis, lattices and lacy gingerbread trim. Here even the doorframe is curved.

RAYMOND WAITES

RAYMOND WAITES

Textural Play

Smooth versus rough; glass transom versus tightly closed shutters—these are the contrasts that keep the eye interested in this Santa Fe doorway.

Doors offer a wealth of visual pleasure. And beauty doesn't occur only in the formal doorway; nor is it exclusively the builder's art. House owners frequently add individual touches to those of the architect or builder. A bright red door, or a doorway wrapped by a garland of flowers, or a door marked by a

Whaler's Pride

The importance of this staunch dwelling and its inhabitants is announced by the Federal doorway and stairway. It adorns a Nantucket residence.

RAYMOND WAITES

BARRY O ROURKE/STOCK MARKET

beautiful wreath all give different messages about the inhabitants.

And nature herself can work magic on a door, weathering the wood to a soft and welcoming texture and color. So even the most rustic of doorways can exert a powerful charm. Many wonderful old doors were made from a single plank of solid wood or several extra-wide ones grooved together. Dec-

Weatherworn

Weather lends a patina to all things. In this rustic farmhouse dwelling, weather has gnarled the paneled door and siding to textural richness.

ades of weather and wear etched them with a rich, natural patina. Yet, it is often the whim of a new owner of an old house to replace such doors. This is a mistake since these aged doors are frequently the most beautiful of all.

Because doorways are so visible and yet so personal, make yours a welcoming sight to those you know as well as to strangers passing by.

Fine Restoration

Shadows emphasize the deep reveals and outline of this Italian-ate doorway in Providence, Rhode Island.

MICHAEL SKOTT

BARRY O'ROURKE/STOCK MARKET

Windows might be called the "eyes" of the house. Through them, the house views the world and its surroundings just as we catch glimpses into the house's inner realm. Over the years, the role and function of windows have changed dramatically. Early settlers were more concerned with conserving heat and protecting themselves from the elements than they were with admiring the view. For centuries there were no windows as we know them today. Glass was not readily available and it was expensive. It was manufactured in this country only rarely until 1739, when Caspar Wistar established the first large scale and successful glasshouse. Until then, oiled

Vine Covered

The owners of this shingled cottage on Long Island can open their classic 12-over-12 window to allow the sweet smell of the ancient wisteria to waft into their house.

Shutters as Accent

Shutters, painted an unconventional bright red, add a cheery note to a small Cape Cod house with tongue-and-groove siding.

RAYMOND WAITES

ROY SCHNEIDER/STOCK MARKET

paper or fabric was a common means of covering the window. Early windows, or "wind holes," were small openings which let in a little air and light, with a shutterlike device to close them up. Because security was also a factor in this country's early years, small windows and tightly drawn shutters with small light slits secured the house from outside attacks.

Industrial Window

A familiar sight in the older sections of cities are the arched windows of warehouses (fast being converted into living lofts) with their tight-fitting shutters.

As America prospered, windows grew in style and importance. Each architectural period found its expression in unique window forms. In Colonial times windows were rather evenly spaced across the front and sides of the house. Because of its scarcity and the difficulty of transporting or manufacturing large

Victorian Oculus

An ornamental window lights the entrance hall of a late 1800s house in the Midwest. The white trim is pleasing against the blue siding.

sheets of glass, individual panes were small: the older the house the smaller (and consequently the more numerous) the panes. In England, houses were taxed if their windows exceeded a certain number and this practice was probably enforced in some of the British colonies.

By Federal times windows grew larger. Twelve-over-twelve paned windows replaced six-over-eight double-sash windows. By Victorian times windows evolved into the four-paned, double-sash windows that are found throughout the country, particularly in the Midwest.

The grander the house, of course, the grander the windows. They are clues to how prosperous or how aspiring were the houses' builders.

Sponge Painting

Dark grey paint is sponged on the wall in a highly unusual polka dot pattern. Window frame repeats the rich charcoal color.

Bonnet Top

The thick adobe walls allow for this unique window detail. The crown treatment and splayed side walls create the interest. No other decoration is necessary.

MICHAEL SKOTT

LISL DENNIS

All architectural periods exhibit great interest and variety in window design. Some of the most beautiful windows date from the late 18th through the 19th century. We have only to visualize the elaborate, lighted doorways of the Georgian mansion, where the side lights and over-window are outlined in delicate tracery to feel a sense of elegance and luxury. The Palladian window, a design imported from Italy via England, is a three-part window capped by a semi-lune over the center. Used extensively through late Colonial and Federal times, it's still one of the most elegant of all window designs.

Sometimes windows have characterized whole cities, stamping them

Blue Window

The three casement windows on these pages are all in the restored Peter Wentz farmhouse, a museum open to the public in Worcester, Pa. Each makes a clear color statement.

Yellow Window

Bright yellow paint frames this window in the Peter Wentz farmstead. Note the unusual—and historic—diamond-and-squiggle pattern beneath the chair rail.

MICHAEL SKOTT

MICHAEL SKOTT

with a unique architectural identity. San Francisco comes to mind. The ubiquitous three part bay window animates the street scene for blocks on end. (Was the bay window so called because it overlooked San Francisco Bay?) The uniform rows of Victorian houses with their projecting bay windows play no small part in that city's reputation for stealing our hearts. Or, think about Nantucket or Cape Cod and you have an immediate image of repetitious windows.

White Wood

Gingerbread trim turns paired windows into a lighthearted valentine.

Adobe

Greek Revival even reached the Southwest. Here is a covered porch with a classical dentil frieze.

Specialized windows through various periods were functional as well as decorative. The charming eyebrow windows, a row of shallow windows located just below the roof line of the story-and-a-half Federal farmhouse, is an example. Attic windows set in the hip roofs also took many delightful forms. The oculus and bull's eye windows, round or oval as the names suggest, were frequently used in the houses' gable ends.

Red Brick

Red might almost be called America's national color. In brick, it characterizes houses, warehouses, and even whole cities.

Classic Contrast

Window trim adds a decorative accent to a clapboard house.

Lighthearted

A romantic farmer proclaimed his love of life from the roof of a Midwestern barn.

Pastel Fretwork

Color comes as an unexpected jolt on this balcony in Virginia. The balustrade is Georgian fretwork.

Climate is another factor which has helped determine size and shape of windows. Harsh New England weather dictated small openings in the house shell, while Southern heat and humidity demanded taller, floor-to-ceiling windows that were as large as doors. In such near-tropical climes, the tall doors could be thrown open all around, inviting breezes indoors. Thus, the French door is the norm in many types of Southern regional architecture, especially in plantation houses.

Snow Graphics

Snow on the pitched roof and shed of this red barn sets up a strong graphic image on the landscape.

Balconies

Flowerboxes on a second-floor balcony brighten the New Orleans street scene.

Here, the living areas are raised to the second level and shaded by wide roof overhangs that act as parasols to deflect heat off the windows.

Houses in the Far West have also evolved window treatments suited to that hot, dry climate. Adobe construction of thick clay walls proved to be an effective shelter against the desert conditions. The thick walls are heated by the sun all day and release that heat slowly at night when the temperatures often drop dramatically. Windows are

Victoriana

Typical Victorian windows are elongated and topped by an arch framed by the straight lintel.

Shadows

Shadows double the impression of a scalloped lintel on a Victorian cottage.

Colonial

Short and wide, the Colonial window is a double sash with symmetrical panes flanked by shutters.

Southwestern

Hatchwork from the plasterer's trowel patterns the walls of a Santa Fe adobe.

typically small and deeply set. They also are shaded by a roof extension that forms a continuous porch, called the portal. This not only acts as a sheltered walkway connecting the building's rooms, but also prevents the direct entry of searing sun and desert winds.

Like the human appendix, shutters are a rudiment from another time and have fallen into disuse. Octogenarians still remember, though, a daily chore they performed as children: in the winter when the sun went down at

French Influence

Tall, floor-to-ceiling windows are part of the street scene in New Orleans.

Mediterranean

Rusticated walls and arches outlining these shuttered windows have a classical symmetry.

night, and in the summer when it became too hot, it was their task to run around the house to close all the window shutters. Window pane glass was notorious for transmitting heat. The shutters kept the sun's heat out at high noon and stopped its loss at night.

Today, shutters are purely decorative. Yet, they are so much a feature of particular period styles that most houses look denuded without them. There is a tendency to

White Target

A bull's-eye painted white on the side of a barn is a target for the eye.

Durable

Shakes were so durable that houses from the 1700s still have their original shake siding.

remove the shutters from old houses when they are being painted—and not to put them back again. Because it is so difficult to locate original shutters (and shutter hardware), owners are far better off keeping their wood shutters in good repair. Once lost, they are almost impossible to replace.

Only in the 20th century has the view become the prime motive for window placement, although it was a consideration in Victorian times. Contemporary houses are specifically sited and

Country Victorian

The ornate lintels, turned brackets and drop finials bear testimony to America's architectural whimsy.

Regional Motifs

Folksy banisters developed according to the skill and whims of local carpenters.

Closed for Siesta

Towns in hot climates generally close down to escape the heat of the noonday sun. Hitching post has a horse head.

Cupolas

The tiny windows and crowning cupola are part of the American farm vernacular.

designed to concentrate on the best aspect of the view. A distant mountain range, a pond or lake, or any other pleasing vista determines both where to place the house on its site and where to put openings in the house envelope. The 20th century also marks the advent of the window comprising a single sheet of glass. This became possible only with air conditioning and central heating. Indeed, the technology that brought us insulating glass and the means to keep the house interior at a comfortable temperature has drastically altered how our houses are built and what they look like. Once windows began to lose their role in temperature control, modern architecture went a step further in losing its regionalism—at a drastic expenditure of energy.

We are, however, beginning to work with nature once again, instead of disregarding her completely in house design. In the future we may see once again the strong regional differences in architecture that occurred in the past.

Color Contrast

Stucco in sandy rose animates this Louisiana facade.

Picket Fence

The modern-day adaptation of the old fortress barricade, the picket fence is as American as apple pie.

Exposed Beams

Vigas, or beams that extend past the stucco walls, are characteristic of adobe construction of the Southwest.

Flags Unfurled

A small town gears up for the Fourth of July parade with flags, bunting and striped window awnings.

Pathways express in eloquent terms the nation's technological and geographic progress. First came the simplest footpaths, a ribbon of green threading through the virgin forest. Sidewalks in small Colonial towns may have been brick lined, like those in Colonial Williamsburg. The first roads were gravel lanes traversed by horsedrawn carriages. And it wasn't

Footpaths

Early byways were often brick-lined. Other footpaths and streets were frequently made of cobblestones.

until the arrival of the automobile that paved thoroughfares became necessary and began to replace the quaint, if soggy, byways. The towns that developed alongside the new roads marked our westward expansion. These towns often had a regional spirit, especially in the early days. Thus, the towns of the Eastern Seaboard are Federal in character with their dignified architecture comprising straight lintels and door-

Roads

The nation's first roads were little more than gravel lanes that, in muddy weather, made travel arduous.

ways and simple lines. Travelling inward, the architecture of the mid-1800s changes to reflect the period of Midwest development, as buildings take on a Victorian air, with porches, gables, ornamented brackets and tall windows. The roadside architecture of the 20th century has a sadder record. Highways across the country are littered with fast-food signs and squat commercial buildings. We are losing the

Highways

Today, the country is crisscrossed by super highways, linking the coasts. One can traverse the country by car in a matter of days.

regionalism that makes our country so diverse and so endlessly fascinating. That's why it is so important to preserve and rehabilitate what little is left. Many do indeed appreciate how important their early architecture is: Providence, Baltimore, Newark, Portsmouth, Savannah, are all examples of towns that fought to reverse the slide into anonymity and turned slums into splendid historical sections.

Runways

In this age of supersonic travel, airplanes connect the four corners of the earth.

BARRY O'ROURKE/STOCK MARKET

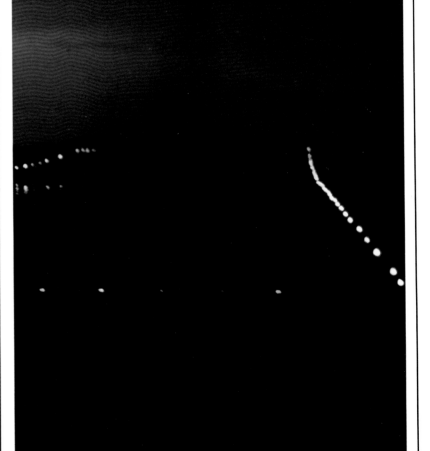

MICHAEL SKOTT

Start with Things You Love

Raymond: Ideas for an entire home can come from the smallest things—a piece of fabric, your favorite quilt, the carpet you're stuck with, or Grandmother's dining table or sofa. I loved the old fabric below and it became "Country Tea" in Gear's first collection. These fabric scraps from an old quilt were the beginning of all the patterns that we developed for the Gear barn. These small prints had the right feeling. They created textures of color rather than strong patterns. I figured that if they worked together in an old quilt they could also be worked together in a room and be mixed in any combination. I did the rooms and it worked easily. I learned in the process that if you keep the color and scale of patterns the same, you can't miss.

Design by Color

These small prints, "Country Basket" and "Salt," have become classics and are still sold. Each year we bring them out in new colors.

Develop a Mood

Faded colors from many washings inspired the color feeling of soft, warm tones, which are so livable. They help you develop your country mood.

Be Confident when Mixing Elements

Fabrics of dots, plaids, and small-scale prints, like those in an old quilt, show you how to mix patterns together. Look at how beautiful they look against the wood of the old pine table.

Tom McCavera

AN AMERICAN DESIGN MOVEMENT: America is still a land where a small business can take root. New Country Gear began only six years ago with just two people, Bettye and Raymond. Bettye was the U.S. manager for Louis Vuitton, an imported French luggage line. Raymond had been with Design Research and Marimekko, two influential sources of contemporary home products. They each wondered why America looked to Europe for design inspiration. The time was ripe for an American point-of-view in design, utilizing American manufacturers. In 1978, they started Gear to manufacture soft-sided luggage with $8,000. Bettye later raised enough capital to cover overhead and they worked at other jobs the first year. Bettye met and married Bill Musham, a successful international businessman in 1979. Bill became Gear's chairman and brought his creative financial ability to the fledgling company which was going through a period of rapid growth and poor cash flow. Six years later, Gear home furnishings have retail sales in excess of $300 million in 1983. You can buy color-coordinated fabrics, wallpapers and home furnishings in your hometown that make your decorating easy. Gear has made an American Design Movement a reality. The American Dream can still come true. 🏠

Raymond Waites, an American designer: When I returned home from working in Europe, I saw America with new eyes. I was homesick. It's amazing how you can miss the taste of a hamburger or a bowl of chili.

One day, I bought an old farmer's bowl. I loved it; it felt warm and friendly. These were purely emotional responses. As a graphic designer, I was trained differently from fabric and interior designers. They design with paint and brushes while I work with a camera and T-square. I had never actually designed a room. I grouped objects I liked on a table for the Gear barn. If I could capture the feeling with these objects, I felt I could expand it into a whole room. I cut out photos from magazines of fixtures, furniture, folk art with a country mood. I pasted them on cardboard. What began as an emotional response became a problem-solving approach to design. These have become "mood boards"— the process I use to design Gear's collections. As we design new products, we build on our American color palette. The colors we introduced our first year still work with those we introduced this year. We work with manufacturers with wide distribution so that you can find the tools you need to design your home wherever you live in America. 🏠

Bettye Martin Musham, an American entrepreneur: It was an ambitious undertaking to start a company that would also become an American Design Movement. It took optimism and a belief in people. It has succeeded. Perhaps this could only happen in America, especially if you are a female in the 1970's. My years representing artists and photographers, and later working for a large advertising agency, had given me insight in relating to people, their talents, and its effective usage.

Raymond had the wonderful combination of imagination and responsibility. It seemed an easy thing to start a company but to run an ongoing business is one of the most difficult tasks one can do. Things you take for granted when working for someone else become momentous obstacles, like having someone answer your phone, take messages, do correspondence. These details have to be done in order to get on to the big things. How do you finance a company? This took friends who believed and who were willing to take risks. Success does breed success. Today, you can find Gear's American designs in shops in Japan, Singapore, Australia and Europe, too. The biggest task was to take an idea and turn it into a reality: Gear's American collections that make your home decorating foolproof.

Norma Skurka, design reporter: Writing a book is one of the most exhilarating things that anyone can do. This one, with Bettye and Raymond, is my fifth book project about design and architecture. For seven years, I reported on home design for The New York Times. I really thought I knew my subject but I have learned more. Most interior designers and architects may be talented but cannot express what they are doing when they design a home and why they do it. Yet, these responses are the key, the essence of making design livable, practical, accessible. What I enjoyed most about Bettye and Raymond was their emotional expressiveness. As a designer, Raymond would not be content with a statement like "suit the room to your personality." He got inside the thinking process, talked about it, let it all out.

Being so basic and relaxed about design has not been done in this way before. Professionals, like lawyers, like to shroud everything in mystery. Designers and architects speak in non-speak. Coming from the mid-west where people tend to be open and friendly, I prefer things said in an understandable manner. I am chauvinistic enough about America to want everyone to live in better, more beautiful ways. It's why I write books on design.

Assemble your Tools

Here are the elements that set the design direction for the Gear barn. They all share a mood of color and country themes. We call this the "mood board," the grouping together of objects on a table to express how a room should feel. It becomes the blueprint for the room's design.

Blue ceramic bird injects blue accent and whimsical touch.

Horn spoons pick up color of the bowl and add a rusty tone.

Magazine clipping shows the right kind of furniture.

"Country Basket" wallpaper is rust-red like the color of old barn siding or a terra-cotta plate.

Creamer with a moose head intro-duces humor.

Tom McCavera

Yellow ware bowls are the first thing I ever collected.

Baskets for hanging from the beams, to use in all ways.

Clipping of home-made golden jams shares the scheme's color and flavor.

Don't forget candles for friendliest, warmest light.

Spatterware bowl brings in brown speckles with yellow.

Salt-glaze stoneware jugs are things to look for.

Fabrics to soften the room are Gear's "Country Daisy," plus stripes and grids in complementary colors for visual variety. All fabrics are by Cohama Riverdale.

THE DESIGN PROCESS

There isn't a book we know that tells you, in terms you can understand, how to create a room you'll love. Ours does. Here is concrete advice. Our suggestions are not ironclad rules. We do not believe in rules. These suggestions are simple tools to help you decide what you like, how to use color, and how to use what you love in your home. Working in the way we outline here may not be everyone's solution to designing rooms. Try it, if you can; our method works.

DESIGN BY COLOR

1 Color is the foundation of this book. It is also the basis around which to design your rooms. Color unifies everything in a room, and it makes decorating decisions easier. You will make fewer mistakes. Here's how to do it.

DISCOVER WHAT YOU LOVE

2 What are the colors that you like? Is it the white of old ironstone, the glow of silver, the red of a patchwork quilt? Is it the blue of export china or old spatterware? Take out the things you own and love. Group them together by color on a tabletop. Notice how color gives a coherence to different shapes, textures, periods, and scale. Study the grouping. Does it appeal to you? If so, what other things work with the collection?

CLIP MAGAZINES

3 Magazines are great sources of ideas. When you see something appealing—an armoire, a fabric, a window treatment—clip it out. Paste the picture in a notebook for your working design portfolio. This becomes your "hope chest" of dreams. Lay these pages alongside the other things you've selected. Do they complement each other in style and mood?

DEVELOP A MOOD

4 Your furnishings and fabrics create the room's mood. Silks and brocades will result in a formal room. Cottons, chintzes, homespun fabrics result in a more relaxed, comfortable one. Think about this as you develop the room's mood. Work heirlooms and other sentimental objects into the plan. Give family photographs, an old rocker, anything with special meaning, a place in your design. These elements make your room unique. If you love country themes and you are an electronics addict, store your equipment in an armoire. Or leave it out amidst the country things, since we do live in the 20th century! Live with the past today. Well designed objects from different times work well together.

BE CONFIDENT, MIX ELEMENTS

5 Follow your taste. Don't let your family and friends talk you out of your ideas. Throughout this book are examples of odd and eccentric things loved by their owners—an amusing ceramic cabbage collection, a stenciled hearth. These objects make wonderfully personal rooms.

DON'T TRY FOR PERFECTION

6 Perfect rooms are intimidating. People don't feel comfortable in them. They look fine in a magazine, but we miss the personal touches that make them real. If a vase has a chip in it or the table is scratched, don't discard it. The baby or the puppy will only add other chips and scratches anyway. Be relaxed about the furnishings in your rooms. Imperfections are often the ingredients of a room's unique style. Own objects that you feel comfortable about using. Too many fineries stay locked in the cupboard until guests arrive. Use what you have and love. That's what a living home is all about.

TEST THE DESIGN

7 Once you've decided on the color, test it on the wall. Paint or wallpaper a section in the color or pattern. Put the table with your objects on it next to the wall. Add a place setting. Now live with this for a few days. You'll see if you tire of it. If not, you are ready for a firm commitment and investment.

DRESS THE ROOM

8 Be on the lookout for the unusual—those unexpected finds at an antique fair or flea market. A pitcher is great for serving wine; a child's wood wagon may become a magazine rack. There's no perfect place for any object. Move your belongings around. Try them in different rooms and different places. Rooms have a life of their own.

CREATE YOUR OWN MOMENTS

9 We cannot duplicate the past. We can only learn from it. We visit museum rooms and historic houses for ideas, but we don't want to live in them. Mix the historic with the modern. We are a nation with relaxed attitudes about living. These attitudes built American Artech.

THE GEAR BARN

Raymond: Bill had owned the barn for eleven years but only when he and Bettye were planning to be married did they think about renovating it. When we first walked into the barn, it was like an attic full of junk. But it also had a wonderful, rustic feeling. The beams were all hand-pegged—there wasn't a nail in them. I had just returned from working with

Have a Plan

Bettye: From the first, we conceived of the barn renovation as a Gear project. It was to be a working laboratory for experimenting with color and pattern, for creating menus, and for holding cooking classes on weekends. Our dream is to add wine classes.

Design Research and Marimekko in Europe and had very modern European ideas. But when I looked up at the beams, I felt that this was an important expression of American design. I was seeing America with new eyes. Bill insisted that the barn be energy efficient but he didn't want the normal solution of insulating and sheetrocking over the interior structure. On the spot, I suggested that we install a greenhouse inside the space so it could be heated but the interior beam structure would

Conserve Energy

Bill: I was concerned that the barn be energy efficient. We investigated solar heat, heat pumps, wind energy, but finally decided that the best way to heat the space was by the three big Russo wood stoves, our version of natural energy.

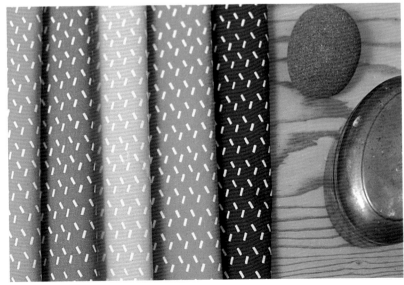

still be visible. Bill liked the idea. It became a designer's dream project. Sometimes an idea can change your life. Bettye, Bill, and I rolled up our sleeves and began to redesign the barn. We all loved the barn's weathered look and blue-gray stone walls and these seemed to set the color direction. But when we looked for suitable fabrics to use, we couldn't find them. Then, while visiting a friend, I saw some fabric scraps from an old quilt. The colors were faded from repeated washings;

Make it Easy

Bettye: It was important that the barn be easy to keep up. It's designed for a way of life where there is no help. We didn't want to get upset if guests came in with wet bathing suits or mud on their feet. This is the easy, relaxed life Americans want.

the small prints had the charm of a floral but were really tiny geometrics. Like those in an old quilt, the different patterns mixed harmoniously. The scraps had the mood, the feeling that seemed right for the barn—very comfortable, relaxed, and warm—a place where you could put your feet up and feel at home. This project was the beginning of all that followed—of the New Country Gear home furnishings collections and Gear's American Design Movement.

Expand in Summer

Bettye: Given the cost of heat today, we use only part of the barn in winter, staying in the kitchen and living room areas. In summer, we expand to the two bedrooms and the sitting area in the lofts and into the crow's nest bedroom under the roof.

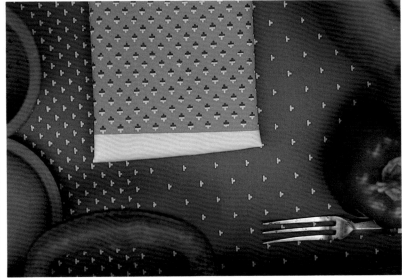

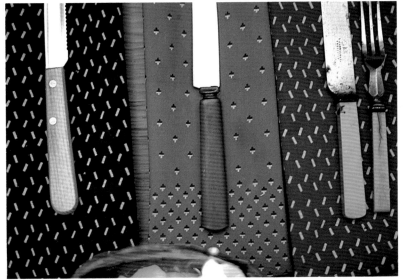

COLOR A HOME

Raymond: A home is more than fabrics and accessories. It's a feeling that you create with all the things you have around you. They reflect who you are and what you love. It's the way you fold a napkin, set your table, make your bed—in other words, it's the way you feather your nest. Here, in the Gear barn, is how it happens. Small prints are used in dif-ferent ways: on a sofa with other prints working together to create a relaxed, country mood; in table settings; on a bed. There is more than one way to use the objects you cherish. If you love something, like a silver spoon, a terracotta plate, a duck decoy, use it all the time in different ways. We can't afford to change our homes every time fashion changes. But we can re-use what we have. Each year, as you add a new piece of silver, or napkins, or sheets, slipcover the sofa, or wallpaper a room, these ele-

Be Inspired

This scrap of old fabric inspired Gear's design of a new print, shown top right. The pattern is Imperial's "Country Buds."

Use Pine

We believe in the importance of mellow wood tones to soften any scheme.

Get the Mood

Terracotta plate, candles, baskets, share the mood of the small print fabric. Each element reinforces the rust color theme.

Set a Table

Even the most informal party, set on paper plates, can be beautiful.

RAYMOND WAITES

TOM McCAVERA

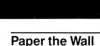

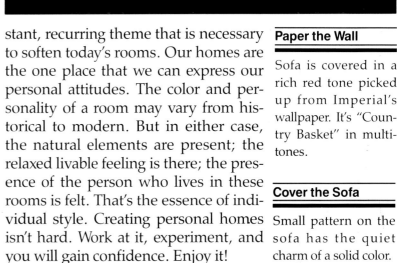

ments can build on the other things you've invested in. This will add richness and complexity to your home and color it with your own touches. Fashion may change—but your personal style only deepens and matures. Our concept of American Artech is taking elements from our own visual vocabulary and using them not only in conventional ways but in innovative ways as well. A universal element in the mix is the warm glow of wood in pine furniture. We believe wood tones to be a con-

stant, recurring theme that is necessary to soften today's rooms. Our homes are the one place that we can express our personal attitudes. The color and personality of a room may vary from historical to modern. But in either case, the natural elements are present; the relaxed livable feeling is there; the presence of the person who lives in these rooms is felt. That's the essence of individual style. Creating personal homes isn't hard. Work at it, experiment, and you will gain confidence. Enjoy it!

Play with Color

Table linens by Leacock, Gear's first licensee, brighten the informal table.

Make the Bed

Springmaid's sheets by Gear put color and pattern on the bed. Pattern is "Country Tea" from Gear's first year's collection.

Paper the Wall

Sofa is covered in a rich red tone picked up from Imperial's wallpaper. It's "Country Basket" in multitones.

Cover the Sofa

Small pattern on the sofa has the quiet charm of a solid color.

RAYMOND WAITES

DAVID RILEY

Field Grasses Dress the Room

Field grasses are tied in a natural sheaf. What could be easier to use and more accessible than the natural things all around us?

Put Together by Color

Pillows mix "Country Basket," "Flower Patch," and "Country Rose," all in the barn rose color family. It all works together.

The Mood Developed

The country mood was set by covering the contemporary sofa with Gear's "Country Basket" fabric. It's easy to use because it works like a solid color; but it has the charm of a print. All fabrics are by Cohama Riverdale.

Charles Nesbit

RED BARNS
RED APPLES

Red hearts, checkerboards, red schoolhouses, red roosters, and cherry red. Red is one of the colors that most characterizes America. Traveling across the country, you'll notice that most barns are red. And in cities, red brick is the dominant building material of most turn-of-the century mills, factories, and warehouses. Reds are fiery, hot, and passionate. Red flowers add excitement to a centerpiece; red placemats and napkins grab attention in a table setting. In a room, red acts like a target for the eye. But while hot reds are best used in small doses, there are also muted reds that are quiet enough to paint on the walls. Certain shades of red are toned down almost to a neutral state. Think of brick red, rust red, the red barn weathered by exposure. Reds mix naturally with anything neutral and, of course, with natural woodgrain. <u>Raymond</u>: I have loved red since I was a small boy, when I bought myself a bright red jacket. I fight it at different times of my life, but my love of red always keeps bubbling up. It's an emotional thing with me. Later on in this book, you will see lots of red used in my city loft. Because it is so powerful, I try to use red as an accent. Color claims you, like objects claim a collector. If you want to know what color you belong to, just look in your closet. Whatever color you find predominant, is your color. (At the moment, there are three red jackets, a red-and-black scarf, a red tweed sports jacket, and a red umbrella

RED

**NATURE'S
BOUNTY**
Apples, dappled
with dew, sig-
nify all the vari-
ety of luscious
reds, greens,
and yellows
from nature's
bounty.

Michael Skott

RED SCHOOLHOUSE

Raymond Waites

Little Red Schoolhouse

Generations of Americans learned the three Rs in little red schoolhouses like this one. These delightful one-room buildings still dot the countryside in rural areas. Located in Sagaponack, Long Island, this schoolhouse has shingle siding, painted red. The white trim makes it all the more vibrant.

Collect Old Silver

Norma: Coin silver was actually made from silver coins, melted down and hammered into flatware by silversmiths. Spoons are the most common and forks are rare. In the late 18th and early 19th centuries it was a note of the family's wealth to own silver flatware. Many people collect coin silver today, and prices for a spoon range from $15 up, depending upon who made it, where it was made, and the condition it's in. Silver by certain silversmiths (such as Paul Revere) commands record prices. Unlike the heavy sterling silver, coin silver is thin and delicate, and feels fragile, although it isn't.

Use it Again

Raymond: In many table details in this book, the same pieces of flatware are used over and over again. This is the way Nancy and I entertain. As you collect the pieces you love, don't leave them in a drawer. Use them. Experiment, mix and match, and improvise with all the tools of the table.

76

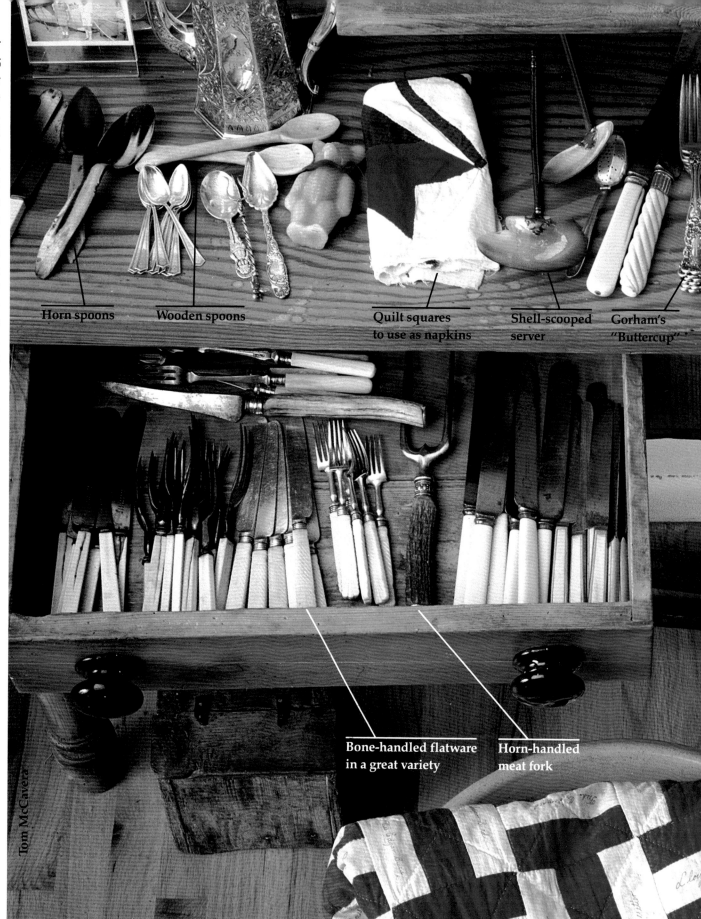

Horn spoons

Wooden spoons

Quilt squares to use as napkins

Shell-scooped server

Gorham's "Buttercup"

Bone-handled flatware in a great variety

Horn-handled meat fork

Tom McCavera

Mother-of-pearl fruit knives

Coin-silver spoons

My favorites:
horn-handled forks

TABLEWARE TOOLS

Nancy Waites: Most of the silver has been part of the family—my great-grandmother got the coin-silver spoons at her wedding in the 1880's and I remember using the sterling at my mother's and Aunt Annie's. We even had a letter from my great-grandfather, George Washington Scott, telling the family where to bury the silver when Sherman was marching toward Atlanta. The pattern is Gorham's "Buttercup" and I now have a service for twenty-four. There are all sorts of strange pieces that aren't made anymore, such as pickle forks, bouillion spoons, and ice cream forks. Some of the silver was never used but now we use it all the time. It's our everyday flatware.

Mix it Up

Raymond: When Nancy and I were married in 1963, we were given the family silver. I wouldn't have chosen such an ornate pattern but as we collected other tableware, we began to mix it all up, using coin-silver spoons with bone- and horn- and mother-of-pearl handled knives that I love and collect. Once Nancy's mother visited us and she was shocked to see such a strange mix on the table. Since she comes from Decatur, Georgia, where things were done in a certain way, she didn't approve of it at all. But over the years she came to understand and love our way of entertaining.

Grain cradle, mid-19th century, is $175.

Canadian goose whirligig is $200.

Old coal sifter is $40.

Turn-of-the-century rug beater costs $25.

Lilo Raymond

Tinware sieve with double handles is $20.

19th-century ember tongs are $100.

Early 1900's rotating toaster, hand-forged iron, is $175.

Antique wooden trough costs $190.

Mid-19th-century tole pitcher and bowl are $200.

Find Old Tools

Marge Brooks, proprietor of Ragged Appleshaw Antiques, Bridgehampton, L.I.: For the most part, our shop specializes in American pine furniture from New England, but we always have a lot of old kitchen implements on hand. They are becoming more popular because of their rustic, primitive appeal. People like to collect objects that are so full of character.

Lilo Raymond

See Hidden Beauty

Sue Bruckner, antiques dealer: I change things around a lot at home. I'll get tired of something or find something that I like better. This collection of kitchen tools hangs on a board in my kitchen. I found the board in the shed out back before I made the shed into my shop. I liked the look of the board, so I drilled holes in it and put in the dowels. Then I stained it to look old.

This hanging box of pine is a mystery. I paid $5 for it and have been offered four times that.

Boot jack is from the early 1800's and has square nails. It costs between $30 and $35.

Revolutionary war canteen is wood with original red paint. Costs about $50.

Wood butter paddles sell for $5 to $40.

Old iron spoon was probably used in a workshop or barn. Costs under $35.

Iron skimmer may have been used for maple syrup, has a rattail handle. Costs up to $50.

Iron skimmer may have skimmed the fat off soap in the making. Costs about $50.

Big dipper for soups or water, may be English, dates from early 1800's. Costs about $35.

A COLLAGE OF QUILTS

Raymond: I bought an old red and white quilt that I loved. Soon, I found that I owned three quilts in red, white, and black. That started this collection of quilts in the same red color range. When I moved into my city loft where the ceilings were twenty-five feet high, I wanted to see and enjoy all my wonderful quilts. I hung them up on two-by-fours as if they were all hanging out on a laundry line. It's a fun idea and a way to emphasize the room's height. It's also a great way to store a quilt collection.

Save a Cupboard

I bought this old cabinet long before we owned this apartment because of the soft gray color. We store Nancy's antique silver tea and coffee service in it. It's always a surprise at dinner parties to open the door of this rustic cabinet and pull out the ornate Victorian silver.

Store Old Quilts

The two-by-fours are fastened to the wall at intervals to allow the display of quilts at different heights. Some are folded shorter than others to give a graphic pattern play.

Bent Rej

Use a Ladder

I use ladders in both the city apartment and country house for displaying things on the rungs. I like the graphic shadows that play on the walls and also the way they accentuate height.

Mass a Collection

I didn't collect ducks—they collected me. I saw eight decoys of the region in a museum shop in New Orleans. They were different in feeling than New England ducks, black with traces of red around the eyes. I had to have them all even though they were fifty dollars each four years ago. I mass them out on a tabletop because their shapes and colors are so wonderful together.

85

Knock-down Bed

Rope beds that came apart were trans-ported across this country by settlers on the move.

Tuck and Fold in New Ways

The wagon bed, top, is waiting for a quick and easy design change. It's accomplished simply by alternating the comforters and folding them in unconventional ways. Take one comforter, for instance, and tuck it in all

around the bed; then lay the other, folded flat or rolled up, at the foot of the bed. With a choice of comforters, the bed can take on a variety of transformations whenever you feel the need for a swift style change. If you purchase sheets and comforters that are related in color, you can change the scheme by the day or week.

Give the Bed a Color Change

The marvelous variety of sheets and comforters has opened up a whole new way to dress the bed. Reversible comforters can give the bed two looks, one that's floral and one that's tailored. Coordinating pillow

shapes, shams, and bolsters also adds to the stylistic variety. Bed dressing is limited only by imagination. Here's what happens when a large-scale floral comforter pairs with a patchwork-style geometric and with a small dot. Use them together in unexpected treatments, such as these.

STORAGE PLATFORM BED

Raymond: We had these Scandinavian chests of drawers from my days at Design Research and couldn't afford to throw them out. We tried placing them against the walls but that just didn't work. Finally, we decided to turn them into a built-in platform for the bed. The frame is covered in laminate. Futons of one hundred percent cotton were just coming in, so we placed the mattress on top of the bed, Japanese-style. Unlike the Japanese, though, we don't roll it up and put it away each day.

Adapt What you Have

The little drawers are good for storing small objects like belts and shirts. You'll notice that there's a lot of red—my color—among the clothing items.

Keep your Pictures Out

Perhaps because Nancy and I are southern, we've always kept our family portraits out. They make a room warm, friendly, and personal.

Bowl of flowers is a red accent.

Bent Rej

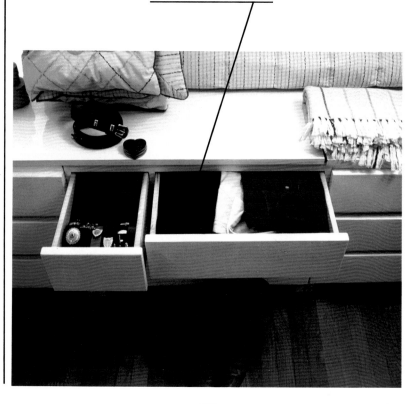

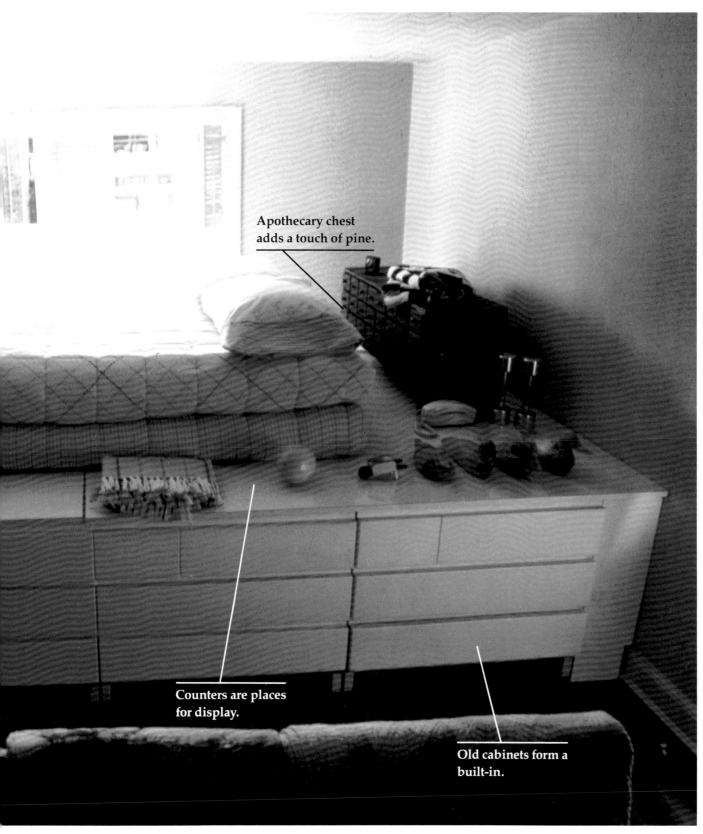

Apothecary chest adds a touch of pine.

Counters are places for display.

Old cabinets form a built-in.

Paper a Wall for Texture

The walls are papered in Gear's textured line, "City Dimensionals," by Imperial Wall-coverings. It gives the surface a texture rather than a pattern, a "soft cloth" look to the wall. How the collection began is a story in itself. We were working with Imperial Wallcoverings and they had these flocking machines they were phasing out. Flocked papers weren't popular. They were about to destroy the old machines. But, I thought, what if we did a collection using that technique to create the look of soft tweeds, herringbone, dotted swiss, wovens, and cloth for walls? I like to think we adapted an old technology for an entirely new wall texture look. For that collection, Gear won the highest industry award, the Roscoe. That's how design is directly related to a manufacturing process.

TOYS

Michael Greenberg, collector: I came from a big family in Brooklyn during the depression. Even as a kid, I saved my nickels and dimes to buy my own toys. Trucks and cars are my passion. The search is everything. I go to yard sales, tag sales, flea markets, country shops. There's a thrill about finding a great toy for a good price. Anyone with a big checkbook can build a collection, but when you don't have a lot to spend, you have to substitute the search for the money. I paid less than a dollar for many of the things you see here—but they represent a lifetime of looking.

Buy What You Love

The toys and trucks are from the '30s and '40s. That's when they were really well made. The cars had real rubber tires and they were good replicas. There's a quality about them you can't find in today's plastic.

94

Wooden roller skates were $1 or $2.

Original Miss Piggy cost a quarter.

Calendar from 1928 was 15 cents and one of the first things Michael ever bought.

Tom McCavera

Horse pulling a sled was $15 a long time ago.

Building blocks are part of a large collection, cost from 25 cents to $50 a set.

Keep Them Out

I built the shelves in the bedroom of my country house for my toys. I like to keep them all out and remember where I bought each one and who was with me. It sets off emotional moments. My toys bridge my childhood, adolescence, and adulthood.

Give a Gift

My father gave us books for presents and I still have my original Horatio Alger books. I keep adding more and giving some out to friends' children on their birthdays.

Move Them Around

I rearrange things all the time. My toys are playthings to me and my house in East Hampton is like my playpen. When I'm expecting guests, I'll spell out their names and "welcome" in building blocks. When they finally notice it, they're surprised.

Paint a Pattern

The painting, the quilts, and the painted checkerboard pattern around the fireplace are vibrant red, the recurrent theme in this personable country bedroom.

Lilo Raymond

Stencil a Quilt

The basic house motif from an old patchwork quilt was interpreted as a stencil pattern on the wall.

BIG RED ROOM

When photographer Hal Davis and his wife converted a schoolhouse in Pine Plains New York, into a weekend place, they made one of its small rooms into their study. The room may be miniscule but it doesn't lack drama. The Davises accentuated the tight quarters by painting the walls a vivid red and using over-scale furniture that's almost too big for the tiny space. Now that's using color and scale with a sure hand.

Tone it Down

Toning down the vibrant red walls is the Davis's collection of dog paintings.

Accent with Rugs

The many tones of the Oriental rug complement the red walls and bring in other colors.

Think Big

The pine cupboard is really too big for the room; and so is this roll-top desk. But that's what gives the space impact.

98

Michael Skott

WORK WITH RED

Many design schemes for rooms begin with the wallpaper. Our advice is, test the scheme. Put the paper on the wall. If it works—do it. A room can be considered like a shoe box with four sides, a lid, and a bottom. Those six planes are the largest area of a room and will dictate the mood and impression right from the start. Earlier on in this book, we explained how to test out a scheme before making a big commitment to it. Gear did just that in this series of vignettes. We wanted to

Freshen with White

Simple red dot pattern on the walls is Gear's "Strawberries," in poppy color. Border is "Strawberry Garland." Chair rail is standard hardware-store molding, hand-painted red and white. Ironstone and industrial lamp are fresh white accents.

test each design concept and see what a room would be like covered in these patterns. The vignettes show a fresh red-and-white strawberry theme, where old pine furniture mixes with white ironstone and a modern industrial lamp, as well as schemes with deeper red colorations and greater drama. Notice how the mood of the vignette alters through the change of patterns. From the fresh country-modern mood of the first vignette, a white ground with a red dot, the mood shifts in the second vignette to a bolder, stronger feeling where a diagonal plaid paper is paired with a red-and-white grid and a big floral-print towel. The

Work on a Grid

Two geometric prints, "Cat's Cradle," and "Homespun," play against each other. Kitchen Gear's "Rosewreath" towel brings in a large floral motif.

TOM McCAVERA

CHARLES NESBIT

100

third vignette is quieter, more traditional in feeling. The last vignette is a geometric grid on a deep red ground. The white lines of the grid give this basically country traditional mood a crispness that is related to the first vignette. To paint or to wallpaper is always the question. There's a place for both and even for a mix of the two where one or more walls are painted and the others papered. If you decide to paint, try painting the walls and the ceilings in the same color. It's more work but it turns the room into a jewel box, an enclosed envelope of color that's nice to walk into. Another trick is to paint or wallpaper only one wall for a color accent.

Deepen for Drama

"Country Daisy," a small-scale print with a cat's-paw motif, is one of Gear's best sellers. In rich berry red tones, it brightens country pine wood accents.

Use Color as the Anchor

Color provides the anchor holding a variety of prints together. Florals, spatter prints, and stripes are linked by the linear quality of the grid wallpaper. All the papers shown are by Imperial Wallcoverings.

TOM McCAVERA

TOM McCAVERA

101

Look for the Unusual

When you look for antiques, choose those with character, like this unusual barrel chair of mellowed pine.

Buy the Best

A fine old comb-back Windsor chair typifies antiques with distinctive personality.

THE GEAR BARN KITCHEN

Raymond: The kitchen in the Gear barn is one of my favorite spaces in the world. It is on the lower level where the cow stalls were. When I first walked into the barn with Bill, it was dark, dingy with a mud floor, but when I looked up I saw this majestic beam, over fifty feet long, and the enormous space. My first thought was to drop an island with lots of counters in the center, whitewash the walls, put in American Olean white tile floors to lighten the space and make it brighter. At one end, we put in laundry appliances and at the other, this huge table that's made out of beams from the barn. Bill and I loved the old iron cow feeders but didn't know what to do with them. When we made the table, we used them as bins at the table's four corners.

Save Energy

Bill: We searched out appliances that save energy and ended up with Caloric and Amana appliances, two American companies devoted to conservation.

Keep it Easy

Bettye: In the kitchen, there is all of the latest technology in a rustic setting: two microwave double ovens, three freezers, and laundry equipment near the back door.

People coming from the pool can drop their towels in the washing machine.

Tom McCavera

Keep it Practical

The barn expresses all the concepts we believe in—it's beautiful, simple, and practical. There are counters for work and display; easy upkeep materials like tile and laminate; good lighting; and all the cooking tools hung within reach.

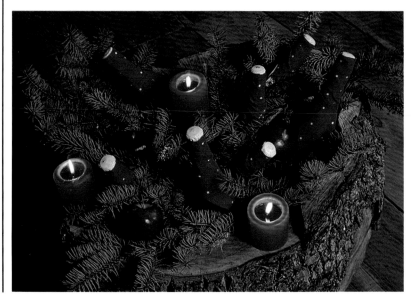

Change with the season

We change the barn with the seasons. When we photographed it here, it was Christmas time and we were preparing for a big party. Bobby Wiggins, a naturalist designer, made all the wreaths and we hung them from a beam and then added a lineup of homemade ginger-bread cookies.

Build a Table

The table was made out of two beams in the barn that had to be replaced. We cut them apart and made the table in two sections, four feet by twelve feet long, using the iron cow feeders at the corners.

Lay it All Out

Foods fresh from the market look so festive and appetizing. I love massing them on the table before we begin to cook, as a cornucopia of color. Some of the foods will go into the meals; others, we used to decorate the tree; and still others, like the apples in the trough, are there all weekend for guests to munch on.

105

BARN CHRISTMAS

Raymond: Green-house panels inside the barn keep in the heat but let you see the wonderful warmth of the wood-beamed ceiling.

Bettye: Baskets are tied in bright, red bows.

Bettye: We used a hollow tree trunk as a big wine cooler.

Tom McCavera

Bobby: Yellow and red fruits and vegetables in baskets are oversized Christmas ornaments.

Trim a Tree

Bettye: Our 20-foot-high Christmas tree came from down the road. Since the tree was too big for ordinary ornaments, Bobby Wiggins used baskets of fruits and vegetables for tree trimmings.

Raymond: Candles everywhere—there never are too many.

VEAL BIRDS HOLIDAY BUFFET

Maxime de la Falaise, food author: At holiday time, from Thanksgiving to New Years, we really don't need an excuse to throw a party. Just getting into the spirit of the season is reason enough to fill the house with family and friends. Theme parties are a good way to unite a group with no common denominator: the theme itself links young and old, new friends with old. The theme for this party was simply trimming the tree. One contingent filled baskets with fruits and vegetables for the tree, while another group helped in the kitchen. Here, we whipped up veal and chicken birds, thinly sliced and filled with cheese and peppers. We made a platter that no one could resist.

Improvise with What You Have

Raymond: These zesty birds dictated the rough, woodsy presentation: a wicker platter garnished with two fat green-and-white leeks with curly tops. The platter was improvised—we stole the top from a wicker basket.

Each bird is sprinkled with extra slices of lemon and red peppers for even more color.

Veal Birds Recipe

Per serving:
1 raw veal scallopine or chicken breast, flattened
pepper, salt
thyme.
1 slice Gruyère or Fontana cheese

2–3 strips red pepper (cut in a circle lengthwise and opened up to a long strip)
1 clove garlic, peeled white sewing thread
Season top side of meat with pepper, salt, thyme.

Lay thin cheese slices on to fit; place pepper strips in center crosswise.

Roll up meat enclosing filling and tie with thread.

Sauté in butter or oil with mixed herbs and garlic to brown, then gently cook through, about 5 minutes.

For red on red: serve with a cold sliced beet salad in vinaigrette with slivers of endive, cut lengthwise, and sprigs of watercress.

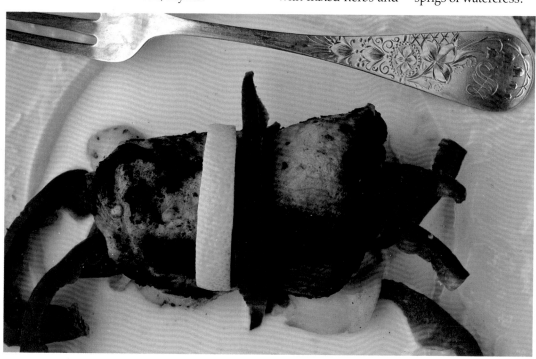

108

HARVEST PILGRIM'S PIE

Maxime: Every season suggests different settings and menus. Spring and summer suggest seashells, moss, and wildflowers to garnish light-hearted meals. In winter, oysters might arrive nestled in tiny snowbanks on the plates; the vodka buried in a block of ice. As fall sails in, the menu responds to autumn's harvest colors and foods are heartier, too. Here's a pilgrim's pie to serve for the holidays. It's a casserole of turkey, carrots, peas, onions, parsnips, and potatoes, containing all the fixings of a real turkey dinner but on a reduced scale for smaller families and ovens. It's also a delicious way to make the most of leftover turkey.

Pilgrim's Pie Recipe

Serves 6
3 lbs turkey breast, cooked
12 small carrots, lightly poached
6 tbs green peas, lightly poached
2 large onions, sliced, sautéed until softened
6 small parsnips, lightly cooked
Enough turkey gravy to cover above ingredients arranged in an oven-proof casserole
Turkey stuffing to cover surface of above ingredients
4 large Idaho potatoes, boiled, mashed with butter, cream, seasonings, and grated nutmeg
4 yellow yams or sweet potatoes, mashed, puréed with butter, seasonings.
12 tiny pearl onions, cooked

3–4 raw cranberries
Several sage or bay leaves

Arrange turkey and vegetables in bottom of casserole or hot pot. Cover with gravy, then with stuffing.

With a pastry bag, decorate the top of the dish with alternating bands of white and yellow purées to make a lattice. Add a band of white mashed potatoes around rim of dish. Fill spaces between lattice with pearl onions interspersed with cranberries. Decorate with 2 small sage or bay leaves.

Reheat in the oven and serve with cranberry sauce and, if you like, a side dish of sautéed or puréed chestnuts.

Serve a Casserole Wreath

Raymond: This casserole, or any casserole or pie, looks extra festive and appetizing when presented with imagination. I placed it on a wooden tray and surrounded it with walnuts, hazelnuts, and cranberries, surrounding the casserole in a harvest wreath.

Horn- and bone-handled flatware mingles with silver spoons.

Candles glimmer
from carved
pumpkins.

Tony McCavera

BEST PUMPKIN PIE

Maxime: The scarlet, purple, gold, yellow, and flaming russet leaves of autumn inspire a menu in the same tones. This color palette is reflected in stews, pies, pastry crusts, brown loaves, apples, and, of course, pumpkin pie—the dessert and perfect ending to our harvest meal. A dash of molasses and splash of bourbon give this pie a touch of class. It's presented like a jewel on an oiled-wood platter ringed with nuts and berries.

Pumpkin Pie Recipe

1 8-inch spring-form pan , lined with crust
1 cup cooked, well-drained pumpkin pulp
2 tbs molasses
3 eggs, well beaten
2 cups milk
¼ tsp salt
1 tsp cinnamon
¼ tsp ginger
¼ tsp grated nutmeg
1 tbs bourbon whiskey

Preheat oven to 350°. Mash pumpkin pulp through a colander or food mill.

Mix pulp with eggs, well beaten, molasses, milk, salt, cinnamon, ginger, nutmeg, and bourbon. (For a lighter pie, the eggs can be separated and the whites, stiffly beaten, folded in at the end.)

Pour mixture into the pie pan and bake for 25–30 minutes. Cool on a rack so that the underside stays crispy.

112

Whole nuts and cranberries add texture and rich browns and reds to this harvest theme.

Tom McCavera

Pearl-handled fruit knives are unexpected touches of elegance.

Work in Harvest Colors

Raymond: This rustic platter is a tree trunk slab that came straight from the lumberyard. It repeats the warm tones of wood used throughout the room. We oiled it to make it useful as a platter. Here it rings the pumpkin pie, but I also use it as a handsome plank for serving meats and grilled river fish.

113

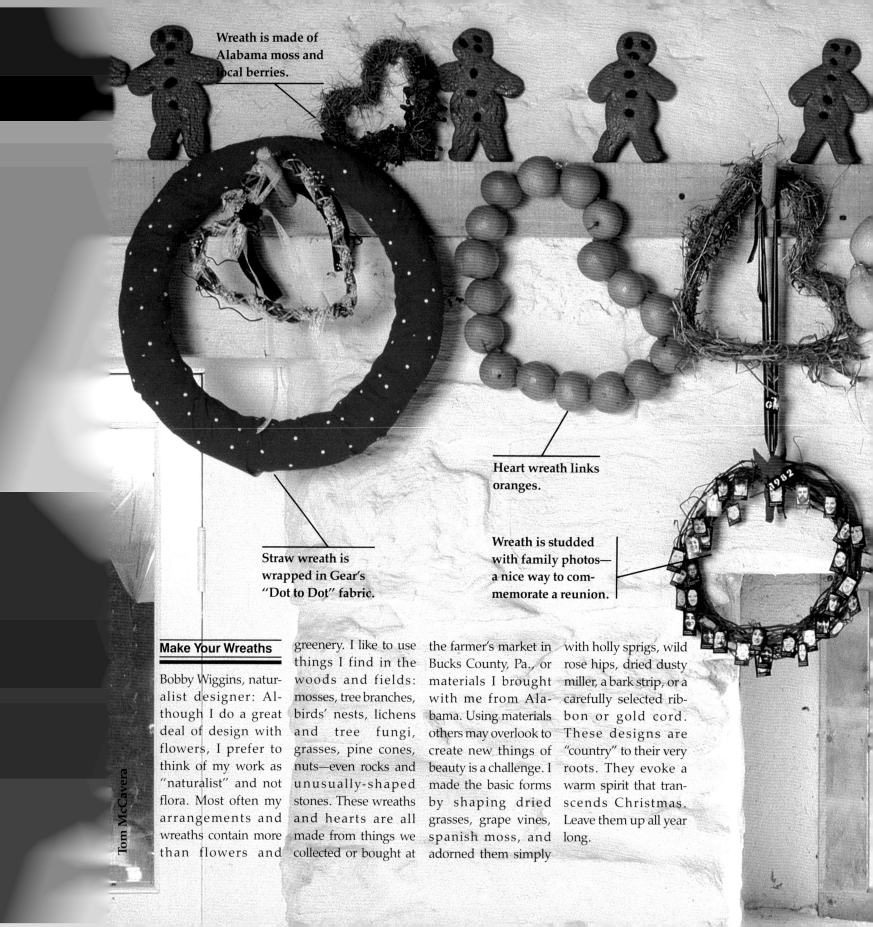

Wreath is made of
Alabama moss and
local berries.

Heart wreath links
oranges.

Straw wreath is
wrapped in Gear's
"Dot to Dot" fabric.

Wreath is studded
with family photos—
a nice way to com-
memorate a reunion.

Tom McCavera

Make Your Wreaths

Bobby Wiggins, natur-
alist designer: Al-
though I do a great
deal of design with
flowers, I prefer to
think of my work as
"naturalist" and not
flora. Most often my
arrangements and
wreaths contain more
than flowers and
greenery. I like to use
things I find in the
woods and fields:
mosses, tree branches,
birds' nests, lichens
and tree fungi,
grasses, pine cones,
nuts—even rocks and
unusually-shaped
stones. These wreaths
and hearts are all
made from things we
collected or bought at
the farmer's market in
Bucks County, Pa., or
materials I brought
with me from Ala-
bama. Using materials
others may overlook to
create new things of
beauty is a challenge. I
made the basic forms
by shaping dried
grasses, grape vines,
spanish moss, and
adorned them simply
with holly sprigs, wild
rose hips, dried dusty
miller, a bark strip, or a
carefully selected rib-
bon or gold cord.
These designs are
"country" to their very
roots. They evoke a
warm spirit that tran-
scends Christmas.
Leave them up all year
long.

Heart wreath is a
string of lemons.

Straw wreath is
banded with Gear's
"Play Grid" fabric.

String of green
apples looks festive.

America in Miniature

Don Zornow, owner, The American Wing Antiques: These dollhouses, bird houses, mailboxes, models, and garden ornaments are all from New England and date from the mid-19th century. They're sometimes called Grandpa's art because grandfathers made them in their spare time for children. They can be very elaborate with gingerbread trim, porches, and turrets. They're getting harder to find and more expensive because so many people are collecting them.

Star-patterned quilt costs about $350–$400.

A little house can cost anywhere from $50 to $1,000.

A YOUNG-AT-HEART PARTY

Maxime de la Falaise, food author: Children's food should be varied and presented imaginatively. If it is, the chances are that children will grow into adults with the eclectic, gourmet tastes that are the spice of life. Even such a mundane thing as a sandwich can be made special and it only takes a few minutes of extra time. This sandwich of nutritious brown bread hiding slices of banana is like a little gingerbread house. The windows and door are cutouts of leftover scraps—cheese, peppers, or even candy. This home is small but it makes for big eating.

Plan a Picnic

Here's another sandwich that's nice to take along for a children's picnic on a crisp, fall day. Finish it off with a dessert of lollipops.

Cornbread Dagwood Sandwich

Mix the contents of a one-pound package of cornbread as directed on the package. Put half the mix in a baking dish and bake for one-half the time indicated. Now you are going to spread the bread with a flavorful filling before baking the remainder so search your refrigerator for any scraps— chicken, gravy, stew. (We filled ours with chili.) Spread the leftovers on top of the partially-cooked bread. Add the other half of the cornbread mix to the pan. Bake the remaining time given on the package recipe, or until a toothpick comes out clean.

Cool, cut in slabs, and wrap in plastic.

Be Playful

Raymond: The little brown-bread house was so whimsical that we turned it into a playful barnyard scene. The house sits in a wood steamer top that makes a pen for toy animals.

TOM McCAVERA

118

Raymond: The toy animals are a collection that has been growing over the years. Bill and Bettye gave me my first little sheep and since then I've been adding to it. I now have a flock of twelve plus a goat. They're fun to plant amidst the food, especially when the guests are young or young at heart.

Sandwich House Recipe

Butter slices of a loaf of brown bread. Spread each with slivers of banana. Pile up the slices into a cube. Up end it. For the house facade, cut out door and windows. Line with red and green pepper scraps or other colorful vegetable slices. Two bread slices make the A-frame roof. The construction is skewered together with toothpicks. A twig is stuck through the roof to the ground as a little tree.

119

PINK HOUSE
ROSE BUDS

Pink ribbons, peonies, piglets, and valentines. Rose and pink are the prettiest colors in nature's palette. Driving down a country road, you'll smile when you come upon a pink house. Nearly all towns seem to have one. Some unpainted adobe buildings in the Southwest and in Louisiana actually take on a shade of dusty rose when tinted by sunshine, since rose is the natural color of certain types of stucco. No longer regarded as strictly feminine colors, muted rose and pink are part of our visual vocabulary, and are being used more freely in the home. Rooms benefit from all the newly popular rose tones and their relatives in the color family: peach, apricot, melon, and terracotta. These tones are flattering to both the room and its occupants. The rosy hues send off a lightness that is livable—and romantic. Rose and its color family are superb mixers. Pink and white is certainly one of the prettiest combinations. But pink also works amicably with all the other pastels, as well as with more subtle naturals, such as stripped pine and even furniture painted in deeper tones, such as those verging on brick and barn red. Nancy Waites: In the south, houses almost always had a pink sitting room. Ours had a settee and side chairs covered in a pink floral fabric. It was considered a proper, Victorian color. The sitting room was a formal parlor that was used only when company came. We, children, were never allowed in there, of course. Raymond did our house in the country in white with pink accents. It's a very easy color to live with. And, pink looks lovely with our old stripped pine furniture.

Find Your Color in Nature

Raymond: I use the camera to see color and design. I began by photographing tulips, going closer with the lens to see more and more color. Only when I felt completely enveloped in the rose color did I feel close enough. These photographs set the mood for my living room: a fresh, happy, clean feeling of white with spots of rose. This way of thinking about pattern is very much like the way historic stencil patterns were developed. It's a wonderful way to see pattern and to begin making color choices for your rooms.

Raymond Waites

Be Casual

I like pine country furniture because it is so relaxed. A few more knicks and scratches doesn't matter. The informality and imperfections set the room's relaxed style. I don't want the worry of caring for museum quality antiques.

Small pillow print is Gear's "Tulip Toss," for Cohama Riverdale.

Tie-tab pillows and duffle pillows are Butterick pattern no. 6048.

Print on sofa cushion is "Dancing Tulip," from the Country Graphics group by Cohama Riverdale.

PINK ON PINE

Tom McCavera

Use Pink on New Wicker

Raymond: I wanted a fresh, modern, relaxed mood in my beach house living room. I like things that move around so I bought wicker modular sofas that repeat the color of the room's natural pine. They're covered in a tulip print, "Great Tulip," by Cohama Riverdale. It's a bigger scale and reverse color of the tulip on the antique daybed, shown on the preceding page. Each spring, I look for geraniums of just the right vibrant shade to make the dusty tones look even more beautiful.

Combine What You Like

Raymond: What I like most about my living room, after the happy color mood, is the combination of slick and technical with country and whimsy. Modernists and traditionalists both feel comfortable here. The furniture placement is formal: two modular groups facing each other, an oversized table between with an antique pine daybed to balance the fireplace. Most other elements are accidental and casually positioned around this architectural plan.

Antique door panel sits on the floor like a giant painting.

Wicker modular sofa covered in super-scale rose-on-white fabric balances both sides of the room.

Vincent Lisanti

Stand a Ladder

Pine ladder, c. 1850, is used as a stand for an ever-growing collection of family photos and loved objects.

Repeat the Color

Antique pine sofa is covered in a positive version of the white-and-rose print. It creates a square of strong color, a solid color volume of rose in the white room.

PATTERN A ROOM

Try it Out

Pink-and-white quilt gave the room's color direction: pine wood ladder reinforces the natural wood of the floor.

Think Natural

Wicker modular sofa introduces a natural element; accessories like family portraits personalize the scheme. Flowers add freshness; soccer ball adds a dash of black.

Raymond: You can't always tell what's right in a room until you try it. Assemble the things you love, the colors, the woods, some of the objects you want to use, and actually try them out in your room. My living room in East Hampton is a contemporary all-white room. A pink-and-white quilt I had purchased at White Horse Antiques, in Quogue, Long Island set the color direction of fresh white and pink accents. I was also influenced by the pink tulip photograph I had taken that you saw earlier. The color seemed so clean and happy. I hung the quilt on the wall. Next I placed an old pine ladder from Balasses House, another local antique shop, in front of it to give the warmth of wood. I moved in the modern wicker modular sofa and threw a tulip print comforter on it for color and pattern. The contrast between the antique pine and the modern modulars had the relaxed feeling I wanted. The warm wood tones made it work. I added more tulip prints in different scales, a large-scale tulip print on the modular; with masking tape, I tried the

TOM McCAVERA

TOM McCAVERA

large-scale grid on the wall. I like to use a geometric plaid with a floral. And I also like seeing old things with new. The contrast adds excitement. The prints worked well with wood accents, family pictures, my decoys, and a big pot of geraniums for a brighter pink color. I tried the same pattern of dancing tulips on the wall in a smaller scale. It was a very exciting combination but too busy to use over the entire room, so I used it on a central wall that divides the house and that could be seen from almost anywhere. The other walls were left white to work simple, clean areas against the excitement of the pattern.

Play with Prints

Pink-and-white wallpaper, "Great Grid," adds dimension to the wall. Sofa is now covered in "Great Tulip," playing a grid against the floral print.

Make a Model

You can actually use a shoe box to create a scaled-down model of your room scheme. Remove one of the box's long sides so you can see into the box. Paint or wallpaper the remaining sides the way you plan to do in the room. Put a small piece of wood down as the floor. Place magazine clippings of other elements for the room into the box. Do they create a harmonious mood?

Learn to Delete

Medium-scale print wallpaper, "Dancing Tulip," introduces too much pattern for the scheme and was used on an adjacent wall instead. Wallpapers are all from Gear's Garden Graphics Collection by Imperial Wallcoverings.

TOM McCAVERA

TOM McCAVERA

ROSE

Raymond Waites

**AMERICAN
ROSE**

A bee's-eye view
of the rosebud
shows its sen-
sual shades of
pink in all their
glory.

PHOTO ARTECH

Raymond: American Artech has two sides: the historic, seen in folk art and country artifacts, and the innovative, an outgrowth of new technology. After building a solid base of country-inspired colors and patterns for Gear, I felt it was time to explore new ideas. Taking our cue from Colonial hand-cut stencils, I developed "Garden Graphics," a pattern group derived from actual photographs of flowers. Each pattern is a translation of a flower photograph into a stencil, which is then printed in a half-tone photoprocessing technique. "Wild Rose," this superscale sheet pattern by Springmaid, is our American Artech.

Pick a Rose

Here is the actual photograph of the rose that became Springmaid's "Wild Rose" sheet pattern. When I began working with the photo stencil process on the "Dancing Tulip" pattern, which you saw on page 126, the colors were put down as flat areas in a technique similar to floor stencilling. With this rose pattern, I wanted to experiment with layers of color to develop a softer, more realistic look on fabric. I don't think that this technique had ever been done on fabric before.

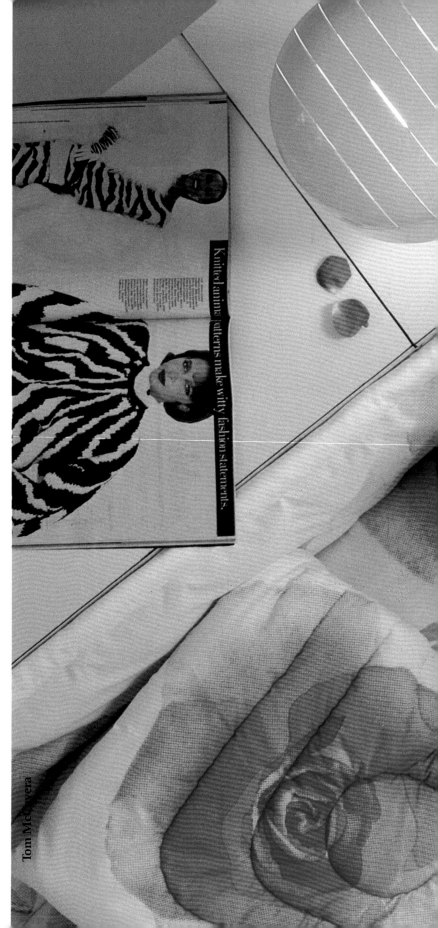

Knitted animal patterns make witty fashion statements.

Tom McCavera

134

DECK DINING

Raymond: My living room in the country is all white with pink accents. Through the window you see the white pool deck and the big blue square of water. These color relationships influence how we entertain by the pool. We take out the big pine country table and chairs from the dining room, set the table with flowers, and serve the food in colorful oversized bowls. Umbrellas bring in touches of pink. So does the food— shrimp, and watermelon for dessert.

Serve in a Wagon

Usually, this little antique wagon holds magazines, but here we've rolled out a lobster catch from the kitchen to poolside. Our friends love it!

Mass Everything for Color

Everything looks better and more dramatic when it's done in masses, like geraniums in a big basket. Simple elements used in large quantities, not arranged but tossed in baskets or their own pots look terrific.

Float a Fantasy

I couldn't resist the plastic duck decoys at a yard sale. They were handpainted by a hunter and cost me $8 each. They are great fun and wonderful pool toys.

Think Pink with Grey and Black

Pearly grey clams, black mussels, pink shrimp, green asparagus, red potatoes, sliced watermelon— it's all served in oversized Hartstone bowls. It looks great and is simple to prepare.

Relate Color Inside and Out

Big umbrellas are covered in the same tulip print that's on the living room sofa. It brings the room's pink color outdoors. The colors inside relate to those outside—pillows, napkins, dishes, can move in and out and always work beautifully together.

Build on Color

Bettye: Three years of New Country Gear patterns build on one another. Barn rose color unites them all, including Hartstone plates in different patterns. Every year, as new patterns are added, the tabletop gets richer and more varied. The table is in the Gear barn kitchen and has cow feeders built into each corner, used in a way the farm's original owner would never expect.

Bed of hay is a nest for mugs.

Cow feeder from
original barn now
holds wine on ice.

David Riley

Lay Color on Color

Raymond: This pink cake is special but the presentation makes it even more so. The Victorian pressed-glass plate encircles the cake like a jewel. We inserted the heirloom forks around the cake for a flash of silver.

Even though the elements are elegant, placing them on a table cover of pink-and-white striped homespun lessens the formality. The hand-written note (in a familiar handwriting) makes a warm birthday greeting.

Put a daisy on the plate for a burst of color.

A tiny gift can wear a big bow.

Happy Birthday Bettye

Antique pickle forks are used for dessert.

A PINK BIRTHDAY CAKE

Maxime de la Falaise, food author: Baking a cake for a friend is an act of love. We made this tempting chocolate almond cake for Bettye's birthday party. It's set on a lacy glass platter and served with antique silver. Even the pink icing under the sugar dusting shines like satin under lace. To make the moment even more special, the individual slice is presented with a pink daisy and the tiniest of gifts with a big pink bow.

Bettye's Cake Recipe

12 portions
1 9" x 3" springform pan wax or baking-paper dry breadcrumbs
6 oz bitter - or semisweet chocolate in small pieces
1½ sticks (6 oz) sweet butter
6 egg yolks
6 egg whites, stiffly beaten with a pinch of salt
¾ cup sugar
6½ oz ground almonds or hazelnuts
2 tbs rum
2 cake racks
raspberry jelly
confectioner's sugar

Place oven rack ⅓ up from bottom. Preheat oven to 375°.

Set the baking pan on the paper, trace a line around with a knife point. Cut out the paper circle, butter it, put in bottom of pan, and dust with breadcrumbs.

Melt the chocolate in a double boiler or bowl set in simmering water.

Once melted, remove from heat, cool.

Cream the butter with an electric mixer, add sugar, then egg yolks, one at a time. Whip at top speed.

At low speed, add chocolate, rum, nuts. Fold in stiff egg whites and when well blended, pour into pan.

Place in oven.

After 20 minutes, reduce heat to 350°; bake 50 mintues.

Remove pan from oven and set on a wet cloth for 15–20 minutes. The cake will shrink somewhat.

Remove side of pan. Invert cake onto rack, remove pan bottom and paper.

Cover with second rack and turn to right side up.

When cool, cover top of cake with raspberry jelly and dust with confectioner's sugar.

Pink Icing Recipe

½ cup granulated sugar
¼ cup water
1 cup sifted confectioner's sugar
liqueur or lemon juice
red food coloring
glacé cherries or fresh berries

Stir sugar and water over heat until dissolved. Reduce heat and boil until syrup—200°–220°F on candy thermometer—or until mixture feels sticky between thumb and finger.

Slowly add confectioner's sugar, stirring with wooden spoon until smooth. Add some liqueur or lemon juice and enough red food coloring to tint pink.

Spread icing on small cakes. Add berry and allow to dry before serving.

141

Victorian goblets can still be found for about $30 for four.

Pearl-handled forks, c. 1890, sell for about $50 for four.

lapping slices of lemon. Sprinkle with paprika.

These decorative mousses can be made with chicken, ham, prosciutto, crab, or lobster pieces (the mold lined with lettuce leaves).

Real Cold Borscht Recipe

8 servings
9 cups water
8 beets, peeled and grated
2 small onions, minced
4 tomatoes (fresh or canned), chopped
5 tbs tomato paste
5 tbs lemon juice
7 tbs sugar

salt to taste
1 small bunch of dill, finely chopped
3 eggs
garnish: sour cream, chopped dill

Simmer the beets, onion, and tomato in the water for 1 hour. Then add the lemon juice, sugar, salt.

Dilute the tomato paste in a few spoon-fuls of soup, then add to pan. Cook 1/2 hour, then cool.

Beat the eggs with a few cups of the soup and return to pan.

Reheat, stirring, without boiling, until soup thickens. Chill.

A brighter color can be achieved by adding some liquid from a can of cooked beets. Stir in dill and serve with a dollop of sour cream sprinkled with dill.

Instant Chilled Borscht Recipe

6–8 servings
2 cans jellied madrilene
1 can cooked beets, drained, julienned
sour cream to taste
a dash of vodka (optional)
pepper, salt
finely minced dill

Whip all ingredients together and chill.

Adapt a Design

Stenciled border around the chair rail and windows is a leaf pattern from an old historic design. You can make your own stencil or order cut-out designs from Adele Bishop, P.O. Box 122, Dorset, Vt.

Mix Old with New

Gear's "Log Cabin" comforter and sheets repeat the pink and green colors of an antique quilt, in softer values.

Put Color Underfoot

New versions of old rag rugs come in lovely pastel colors. This one is hand-loomed. An eight-by-ten rug costs $600 at White Horse Antiques, Quogue, Long Island. Another source is Marian Miller, Inc., 148 East 28th St., New York, N.Y.

Tom McCavera

SHEET DESIGN

Bettye: It's hardly news anymore that sheets make wonderful decorating fabrics. Because of their extra width and length many items such as curtains, round table cloths and runners, lamp shades, and quilt covers are easier to make with little or no seams. The nation's top designers have all had a hand in sheet designs so there is always a harvest of patterns to choose from. Sheet patterns come and go in stores quickly. If you choose a particular design to build a scheme on, stock up on spares. Chances are when you need replacements, they'll be long gone.

Sew it Yourself

Gear has teamed up with Butterick Patterns for many sewing ideas you can do yourself. Tie-back curtains, Pattern No. 6050, is one of twelve patterns of home furnishings you can make. Others include shades, bathroom and closet accessories, pillows, baby items, and tote bags.

Find a Great Bed

Norma: This country bedroom's charm comes mostly from the bed—an antique tester with a gracefully arched top. The curve of the hoop was so handsome that we didn't want to cover it up (a fishnet canopy would be the accepted thing to do). Instead we tied bundles of fragrant spring herbs like garlands with colorful bows and hung them from the hoop. The hot pink ribbons are a bright accent for all of the room's dusty rose tones.

Channel a Quilt

The quilt is extra fluffy and high—a look we love. It's easy to make. This one is made of wide strips of Gear fabrics sewn together and then channel quilted. The dusty color, Barn Rose, holds all the patterns together.

Charles Nesbit

PINE CONES
FIELD FLOWERS

Seashells, baskets, old wood beams, homespun linens and muslin, stripped pine furniture. Naturals are all around us. These muted tones are warm, familiar, and evocative of bygone times when everything was made by hand. Natural elements bring texture and character to a color scheme. They also soften and smooth the hard edges of modern spaces. Naturals are foolproof for color schemes. They provide a neutral background for the livelier colors, blending and balancing the brighter hues, and thereby intensifying their beauty. The most humble objects, a collection of pine cones or a bowl of seashells, for instance, lend a subtle beauty to a room. Natural pine furniture is a recurring theme throughout this book. Pine against stucco and plaster lends a mellow warmth that permeates a room. White, too, creates the most sophisticated of schemes. White-on-white used as a no-color theme continues to be a favorite choice for people, especially those who work with color all day. New England towns, where all the houses—and the village church—are white, are a cherished part of our American architectural heritage. Norma:I am a true "naturals" person. When I looked for my first country home, I was drawn not to the seashore, but to the woods, the meadows, the cornfields where neat rows of growing plants pattern the rolling hills, where cows dot the landscape. I was obviously overwhelmed with nostalgia for the Michigan farmland where I grew up. The sight of cultivated fields and dairyland makes me feel that all's right with the world. I even tend to wear white and beige clothes most of the time. I just feel that they are flattering. Every living room I've ever had was either white or off-white. My latest living room is a beautiful tone of vanilla, white with a hint of yellow-beige. (Even my two puppies are "naturals," one is white and the other is beige.) Rooms of natural tones make

NATURALS

**FIELDS OF
FLOWERS**

Nature leads
the way in com-
bining colors.
Fieldflowers
and grasses
regale in their
infinite grada-
tions of natural
tones.

Raymond Waites

NEW BARN C. 1980

Michael Skott

Move a Barn

Martha Stewart, food author and caterer: I saw an ad in the paper for an old barn and bought it as a birthday present for my husband, Andy. It was taken apart, each piece was numbered, and moved to our property in Connecticut. Andy and my brother re-erected it and put in the big windows. It's a wonderful studio and great for parties.

Light and Air

Coming from industrialized Manchester, Mother Ann advocated fresh air and ventilation—hence the large, uncurtained windows of Shaker buildings.

Ingenious Storage

Shakers hung chairs on pegs around the room so the space could be effectively swept, and to leave room for the "shaking" or dancing that played a role in their religious ritual.

Superb Craftsmanship

Shaker chairs are masterpieces of delicate proportions and comfort. Since there was no decoration to hide flaws, the workmanship had to be perfect.

Spare and Pure

Shaker furniture is exceptionally clean and elegant in line. It looks surprisingly modern.

Old Porch Rocker

Rockers were a uniquely American development. Not only the Shakers made them, so did other country craftsmen. The Brumby rocker, shown here, is still a fixture on front porches.

SIMPLE AND EASY

Shakers regarded work as a form of worship. This religious community was founded by Mother Ann Lee, who, in 1774, left Manchester, England on the *Mariah* with eight followers. At its height, there were 18 Shaker colonies with about 6,000 members. They were superb artisans, and furniture making was their chief industry. By 1830, Shaker-made chairs and rockers were sought after as the finest seating made in America.

BOB WOODWARD/STOCK MARKET

SEASHORE COLORS

This dining room's color scheme of warm naturals with black accents, was inspired by two elements: seashells from nearby beaches and wooden decoys. Located on Figure Eight Island, North Carolina, this weekend house belongs to Ben and Bonnie Helms, both incurable collectors. Bonnie picks up shells off the beaches, and Ben collects wooden decoys from local antique shops. The colors of these "finds" are especially important to them, so much so that they asked Raymond to create a room around the natural colors seen in their collections. The new items they continue to acquire simply enhance the room.

RAYMOND WAITES

RAYMOND WAITES

Use Black for Contrast

Until Ben finds the additional antique chairs he's searching for—like the one in the foreground—the handsome antique table is surrounded by inexpensive chairs that have been stained black. The pickled white floor, expertly done to let the grain show through, offers a clean, fresh counterpoint to the mellow old pine table and arm chairs. The black side chairs provide a dramatic contrast.

Display Your Treasures

The open shelves, pickled white, are an excellent foil for the colors of the pottery and jugs, and make a super showcase for the unusual shapes of the wooden decoys.

Raymond Waites

Mix Different Styles

A single antique chair is easy to find. A matched set is much rarer—and expensive. Remember that chairs don't have to match. This antique arrow-back armchair is used with Windsor reproductions. The copies come in natural wood; here they have been stained to give them the look of greater age.

Yellow pumpkins complement the brown and gold of the plate.

Horn spoon brings in ivory striations.

Tom McCavera

COLLECTING BY COLOR

Raymond: Collecting unmatched china can become a diary of one's life: each piece represents a moment in the past, a special trip, a discovery, a loving gift, pleasure in a single object for its own sake or for the craft that was expended on it. I tend to collect by color. I found this unusual plate in an antique shop and liked its decal transfer decoration: a schooner in the plate's center, rimmed by the russet borders, which are so much a part of English china. These brown and golden tones started my collection of dinnerware in similar or complementary colors.

Line a Plate

This terracotta plate cost $2 at Conrans. This solid color can be laid on top of the more ornate English bone china. Although I love decorative plates, like the one opposite, I dislike putting food on the fussy pattern. The terracotta plates give visual calm for the food, showing it to best advantage. See how lovely the yellow peppers look upon it.

Change at Courses

I like to bring in a change of color at different courses of the meal. The green Majolica plate introduces a strong, green color statement. Because the color is so vivid, I think about the foods that will go with it. Pumpkin cakes are a color complement.

Add Metallic Touches

I think of copper pots and pans as a natural extension of the russet and gold color theme of the plates. We also use restaurant ware pots and bring them right to the table.

End Elegantly

For fifteen years after Nancy and I were married, I hid her family's chocolate service away. I far preferred sleek, modern designs of Italy and Scandinavia. Recently, I've done an about face. Now I like the opulence of the cups and saucers. We end the meal with coffee in these examples of Victorian fancy.

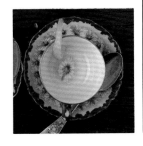

163

**Let Your Taste Be
Your Guide**

Turn-of-the-century
flatware like this
three-pronged fork
can still be found.
Don't let the fact that it
can't go into a dish-
washer deter you
from buying and
using it.

A Spontaneous Touch

The most casual flower arrangement can be elegant. Toss a bunch of narcissus in an old canning jar. This unstudied arrangement adds a personal accent to your table.

A NATURAL WAY TO ENTERTAIN

When Raymond and his wife, Nancy, entertain, Nancy cooks and Raymond adds the finishing touches to the table. They rarely set the table in the same way twice. First, they decide on the menu, and then they delve into the cornucopia of tablewares that they have collected over the years.

For a party in their country home in East Hampton, Long Island, the setting might include earthenware plates they found in New Mexico, an eclectic mix of flatware, and napkins made from mattress ticking. "At first, Nancy's mother was shocked because nothing matched," said Raymond. "But we love to collect things and we want to use them all."

Use What You Have

Don't worry if you have a set of antique spoons but no matching forks or knives. Use them anyway. These heirloom spoons belonged to Nancy's grandmother. Their owners' pride and joy, she mixes them here with flea market silverplate knives and horn-handled forks.

Look for Good Buys

An old railway bench, the kind found in waiting rooms of small-town train stations, makes a fine dining room settle. This one came from The Wrecking Bar in Atlanta and, in 1982, cost less than $100. Great buys can still be found by the scavenger with a sophisticated eye.

Collect on Vacation

Traveling often turns up unusual things for the table. These earthenware plates were found on a trip through New Mexico at a craftsman's pottery shop.

Simple Chairs

Like tableware, seating is more interesting when it doesn't match. Rush-seated Mexican chairs cost $25 when purchased in 1964 and are still sold in stores today. But they are more expensive. (That's inflation.)

ROBERT GRANT

WHIMSICAL

Country furniture is probably one of the most popular of today's decorating choices. And no wonder. It takes the anonymity out of modern, unimaginative spaces and gives rooms warmth and style. There are many ways to design around country pieces, and we see the best in this charming dining room in a California house: All of the furniture is large in scale, rustic woods are mixed with painted pieces, and toys add humorous accents.

Elyse Lewin

Be Bold

A large part of this room's country charm stems from the fanciful accessories. The toy horse is really too big for the table top. But it is exactly its bold size that makes it work.

Repeat the Color

Color is used judiciously to complement all the rustic wood tones. The blue-and-white rug repeats the room's other blue accents, such as the painted chest beneath the window.

Accent with Art

Antique portraits have lots of character. The pose of the body and expression of the face add intrigue to the space.

NATURALS: BASKETS

Elyse Lewin

Dine by Candlelight
An 18th-century chandelier is sometimes better than one that's electrified. The table is bathed in candle glow.

Concentrate on Form
Folk-art objects make delightful substitutes for paintings when hung on the wall.

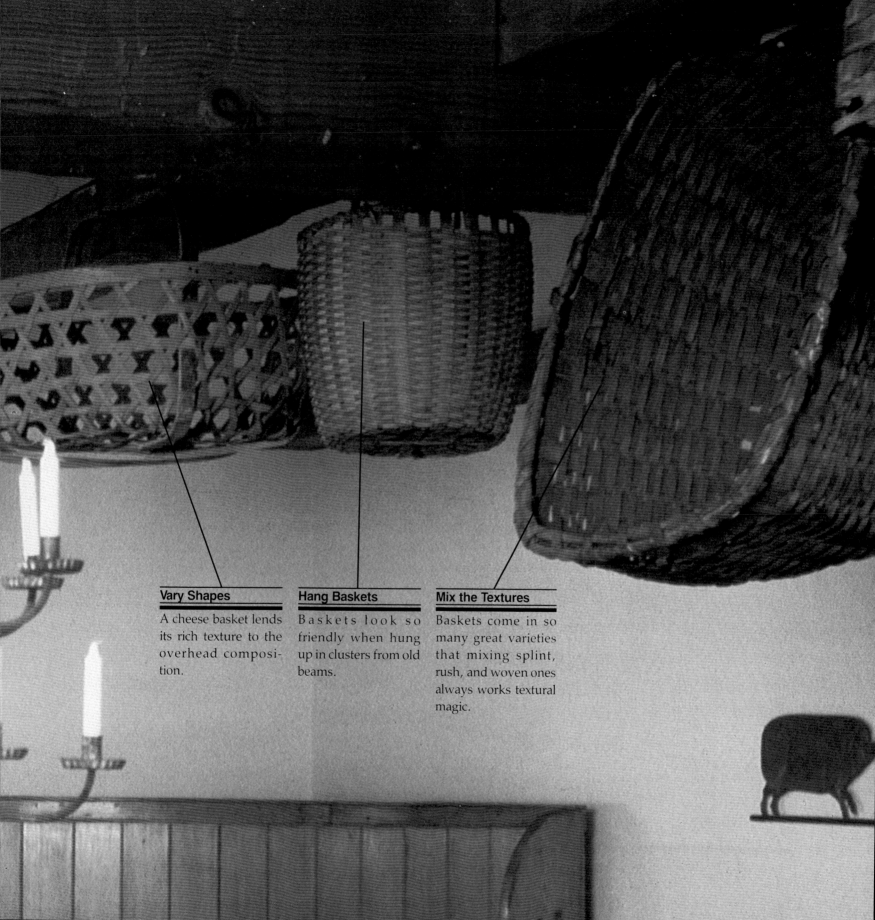

Vary Shapes

A cheese basket lends its rich texture to the overhead composition.

Hang Baskets

Baskets look so friendly when hung up in clusters from old beams.

Mix the Textures

Baskets come in so many great varieties that mixing splint, rush, and woven ones always works textural magic.

WARM WHITE

Peri Wolfman, co-owner, Wolfman-Gold & Good Company, New York City. I like the clean purity of white china. Even the large platters and heavy bowls have a sculptural quality. Living in New York where things tend to look grimy, it's nice to walk into a serene household of all white. Charles Gold and I opened our first shop in Soho in 1981. The store is eclectic; we have a selection that runs from restaurant ware up to fine, French porcelain. Most of it is white because it is so versatile. White china crosses over and mixes with antique or modern, such as spatterware and spongeware; and it translates into both old reproductions and ultra-modern designs. Obviously, people respond to our concept because we have since opened our second shop on the upper east side of Manhattan.

Mix it Up

Our shop sells furniture and accessories as well as the white china: glassware, flatware, both new and antique, old table linens and imported linens, as well as the whole variety of platters and serving pieces. We even sell the old holophane light fixtures. The glass domes are over 100 years old and we update them with new brass fittings.

Michael Skott

170

Convert a Space

The shop is in an old factory which we had to convert. We chose SoHo as the location because it is a growing area with a flavor all its own. People come down to look at the art galleries and little boutiques, where they might find the special and unusual. They are open to new ideas.

Make it Homey

We set the store up to feel like a home. Customers who come in to shop should feel like our guests coming to dinner. We mixed in country antiques, like the big pine tables and country cupboards. That's what the "Good Company" in our shop name signifies.

171

Leave It Out

Open shelves do keep everything out and handy. But they also make more demands on our storage habits. The key is to select and purchase everything in a single color. That way, objects always go back in their proper order.

Group One Color

Grouping items all in a single color is such an easy concept with such dramatic results, that we wonder why it isn't done automatically. Here, the play of china with glassware shows off the contrast of sizes, shapes, and textures.

White cups have their own niche.

Big bowls have a taller shelf.

Baskets are grouped on the top shelf.

Wine glasses slip into drying racks beneath the shelf.

Michael Skott

COOL WHITE

White color schemes are highly sophisticated. People who work around color all day often prefer to live in a serene, white environment. This is the pantry area of Peri Wolfman's kitchen in New York City. As we have seen from her shop on the preceding page, white items are her favorites. White environments are cool, congenial, reflective, timeless. They always look crisp, clean, and orderly.

Think No-Color

Although white is actually the absence of all color, it can be one of the most powerful elements in a color scheme. It cannot clash with other hues but acts as a perfect foil for them. When you tire of the scheme, you merely have to change the color of the accessories to have a new look.

Ironstone pitcher would cost between $10 and $35 today.

Mustard jar came from the grocery store with mustard.

Ceramic canisters are turned around so you can't see the blue lettering on the front.

Old watering can was less than $1 at a tag sale.

Mass It Together

Taking all the white objects scattered around the room and massing them together concentrates color impact in one area.

Chamber pot has a chip, cost about $5.

Collect By Color

Michael Greenberg, collector: My crockery collection spans 100 years. Some things are old, like the dough jar, c. 1880, and others are new, like the mustard jar, c. 1980. A lot of people won't buy something that's chipped or scratched. That chip or crack is often what makes it for me. There's still a lot of life in damaged things. If nothing that you collect is perfect, there's a consistency and a patina that everything shares and it can be wonderful. There's a chemistry about collecting, a feeling that something belongs to you and you connect with it. It's very individual. I like old dilapidated things that other people throw away. I cherish them.

Cow pitcher is about $10 new.

Enameled tea pot was less than $1 at a yard sale.

Lilo Raymond

HANDMADE HOME

Tommy Simpson, woodworker: The house looks and feels handmade, as if it were worked by hand. Missy and I did lots ourselves, scrounging around for materials and getting other people to make things for us. We'd find a potter to make plates or an ironworker to make hardware. We used old scraps, beams from old barns, siding from outhouses and reused things like the settlers did. It's what America is about. Time was when you couldn't pick up the phone and dial the carpenter, you had to go down the road and ask your neighbor for help. It makes the house a partnership of artisans and artists and makes us feel like we're knit into the community.

Work With Nature

I work organically. I like to feel the life and movement in wood. I used ash for strength in the chairs and English oak for character. It's not like Stickley furniture that's square and static. There's a nice asymmetry about them.

Weave Your Own Rug

Missy Stevens, a weaver, made the rag runner. It is worked in a traditional manner on a loom, but done in modern colors, adapting old patterns. It took about two weeks to weave.

176

Teapots line a shelf on high, like an old plate rack.

Handmade chairs would sell for $700 apiece.

Welcome Home hooked rug is probably late 1800's from Pennsylvania.

Lilo Raymond

Find Native Woods

The summer beam came from a barn in Bethlehem, Conn., and the chestnut beams from a barn near Windsor. The ceiling was the siding from an outbuilding near New Milford. One beam has the maker's name carved on it: "L.B. Dane, 1843." We put that up where we can still see it.

Make New-Old Doors

I made the doors of bird's-eye maple panels in cherry frames. The lower panels are spalted maple, part of a tree trunk just before it turned rotten. But that's what gives it the wonderful black lines and graining.

Use Nature's Forms

I'm always looking for unusual wood, like the English oak used in the table. I keep asking, but only one time in a hundred will someone actually have it. This wood was bought for church work in 1932 and lay in an attic in Byram, Conn., for fifty years. There are two planks butterflied together for the top and one plank used for the stretcher.

177

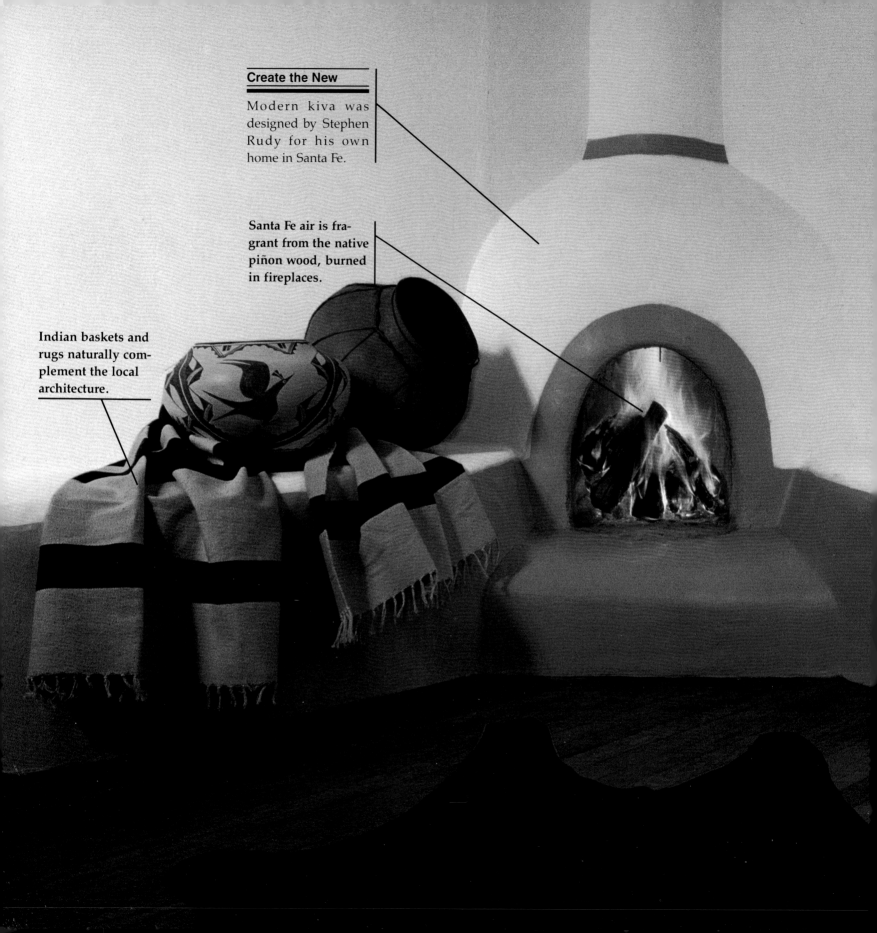

Create the New

Modern kiva was designed by Stephen Rudy for his own home in Santa Fe.

Santa Fe air is fragrant from the native piñon wood, burned in fireplaces.

Indian baskets and rugs naturally complement the local architecture.

Lisl Dennis

NATIVE ADOBE FIREPLACES

Corner fireplaces are one of the most charming and characteristic features of adobe buildings. Called kivas, they derive from local Pueblo Indian traditions and were of great religious significance in prehistoric times, symbolizing home, warmth, and womb. When the Spanish settled in the region, they adapted the custom of putting fireplaces in the corners of their buildings to provide a very efficient way to heat the thick-walled adobe rooms. Here a contemporary kiva—a marvelous example of building for today on old traditions—is shown next to one that was built a century ago.

Keep the Old

This 100-year-old corner kiva is in a restored adobe that is now the Smith Stewart Gallery.

Add Texture with Wallpaper

Gear's grid wallpaper gives a subtle texture to the white environment. It's from the City Dimensionals collection by Imperial.

Build a Bench

Raymond designed the pickled pine benches and they're great for setting out fresh beach towels, baskets of daisies, or just for dropping groceries.

Clamp-on spots are a simple lighting idea, and they can be moved around.

Plan a Seafood Spread

Gear's Hartstone plates and bowls pick up the black and grey tones of oysters and clams. They're big enough to be lap trays. Kitchen Gear towels also repeat the color theme. Masses of yellow squash in a basket are used instead of flowers.

Tom McCavera

We bought the carpenter's bench for $25, stripped it down, and refinished it.

180

Cream pitcher with a moose head is a fun touch from our collection.

Kitchen Gear towels repeat the color theme.

Fresh oysters are served in a big wooden bowl.

GRAND WELCOME

Bonnie and Ben Helms, Gear manufacturers of wood products: When we were building our beach house in Figure Eight Island, North Carolina, Raymond looked at the plan and saw that it was almost a square. The entrance and garage were on the ground level, while the kitchen, living room, and bedrooms were raised a story to get a view of the inlet and ocean. He suggested giving people a grand welcome when they open the front door. That's how the six-foot-wide staircase came about. The front wall is all glass, framing the view like a painting. One sees four strips of color: the beige of the sand, the blue inlet, the green marsh grasses, and, finally, the band of blue sky.

Throw a Party

Ben: When we enlarged the stairwell, we got an unexpected bonus: a great place to spread out a buffet. The sliding glass doors lead to the patio. Since we live by the sea, the menu is often clams, shrimp, crabs, or oysters—set out in a tempting array on an old carpenter's bench beneath the stairs.

TOM McCAVERA

181

Laminate-faced sofa units have open shelves all around the back to store dishes, glassware, books—anything.

Robert Grant

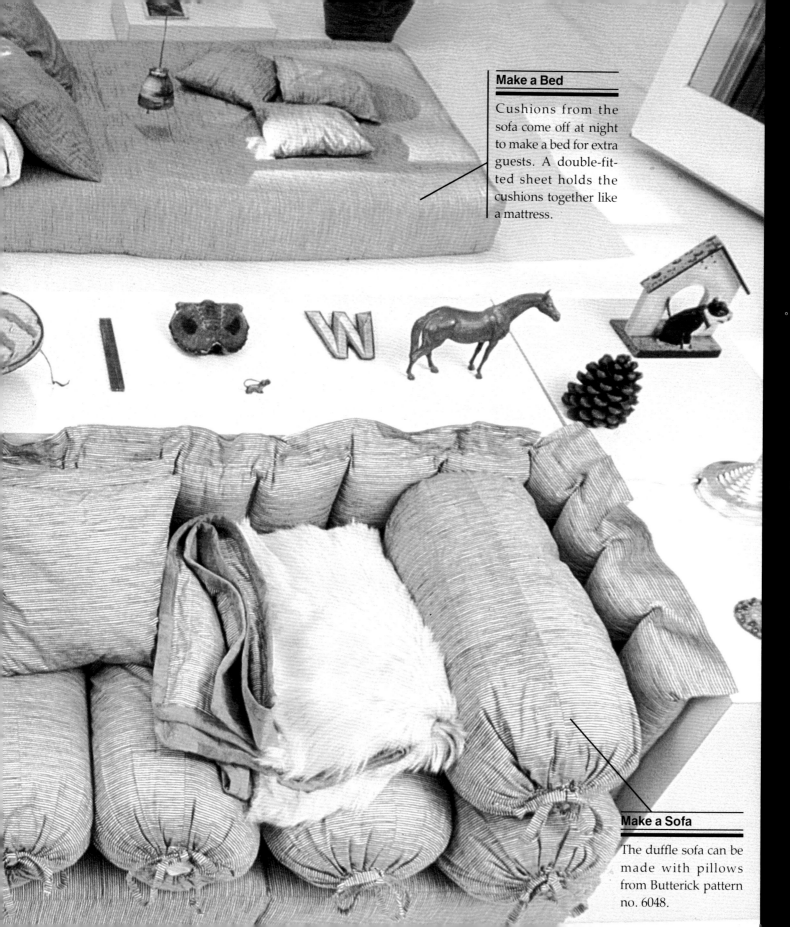

Make a Bed

Cushions from the sofa come off at night to make a bed for extra guests. A double-fitted sheet holds the cushions together like a mattress.

Make a Sofa

The duffle sofa can be made with pillows from Butterick pattern no. 6048.

CHANGE
Raymond
change th
to suit my
and need
sofa make
bed; the c
are a rotat
display fo
favorite ob

WHITE AND BARNWOOD

Lilo Raymond

Handmade truck was
bought at a yard sale.

Fridge is faced in
barn siding.

Vegetables contribute
burst of seasonal
color.

Barnwood paneling
was scavenged
around town.

Shelf is made from old picket fences.

Salvage the Wood

Michael Greenberg, collector: I scavenged most of the wood siding for my kitchen from old sheds and buildings being torn down. Old weathered wood is especially beautiful to me. I love its soft grey color and gnarled quality.

Whimsy

This enchanting farmstead illustrates the playfulness of America's builders. It sits on a street in Monroe, Michigan, amidst more recent—and much more serious—neighboring houses.

Riotous Trim

Wood carvings for house trim ran the riot of scallops and curlicues around the turn of the century. Here, the scalloped trim animates the porch; its lacy edge contrasts sharply with the pointed picket fence.

Howard Kaplan

BLUE DOOR
BLUE SKY

Blueberries, bluebells, blue eyes, cornflowers, bluebirds, blue moon, blue jeans. Blue is the favorite color of most people. Perhaps it's because the two largest expanses of our world are blue: the blue sky and the blue oceans. In combination with white, blue is a dominant theme in the arts of many cultures. One need only think of the 18th-century Chinese export ware that is still avidly collected. Blue has always been a color rich in historic associations. In our own heritage, there is blue-and-white spatterware, homespun coverlets, and blue-and-white salt-glaze slipware. Blue is also special to Americans because it colors a corner of our flag. The uniforms of Yankee soldiers, you'll remember, were blue. In Colonial times, a house with a blue door meant that marriageable daughters lived inside. Schemes that build on the blue spectrum tend to soothe and relax. Blue rooms, whether in the lighter hues or darker shades, are always inviting, sheltering, welcoming. Navy blue happens to be the nation's number one choice as wallpaper background color. Jo Ann Barwick, editor of *House Beautiful* magazine: It's true that I love blue in all its facets. No other color can match the joy it gives me. It reminds me of so many of my favorite things: sky, sea, light, the south of France, Greece. I'm a natural water person. I get a lift from being near the water. I love swimming, boating, fishing, and, most of all, floating on a raft and getting lost in the blend of sea and sky. When you're truly passionate about a color, it makes you feel good. Blue smiles at me. All the houses I've ever had are blue with white accents, or blue with rose or peach or lavender. I'm also a little dippy about blue-and-white porcelain. Is it possible that blue-eyed people identify more with blue?

BLUE

HEAVENLY
The translucent blue of the sky makes our spirit soar—no wonder that's where heaven is.

Mirror on Pegs

The simple technique of placing pegs all around the room unites all the hanging objects in a common design theme. Use pegs to hang a mirror.

Lilo Raymond

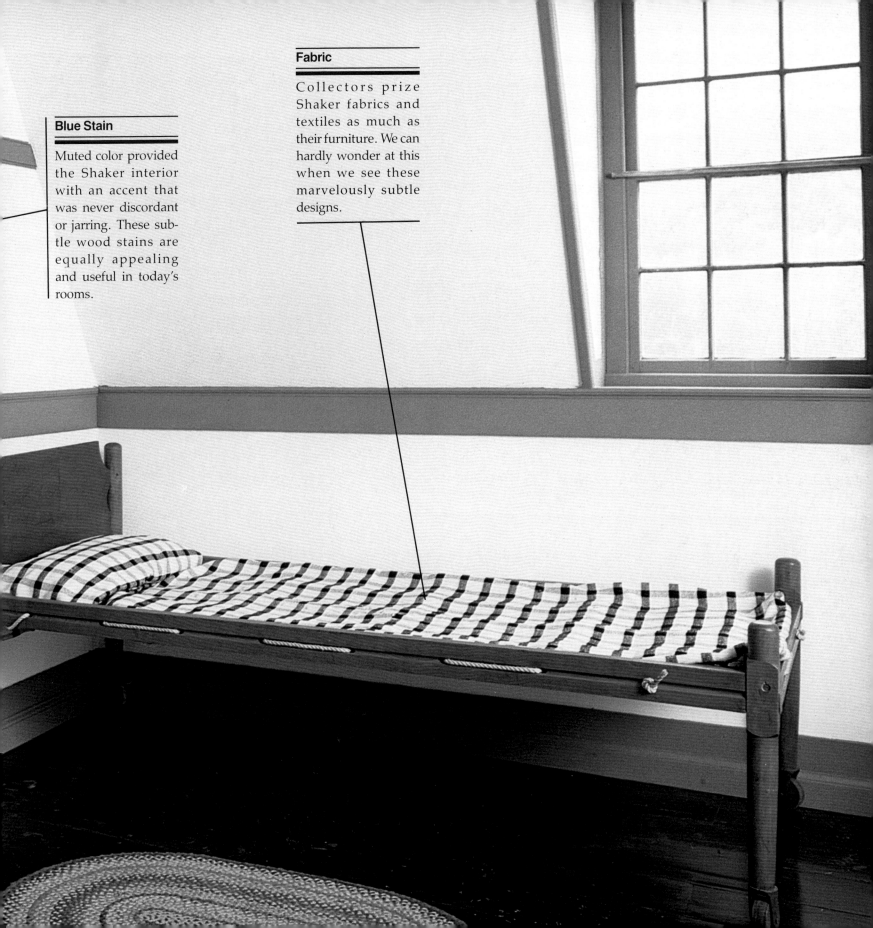

Blue Stain

Muted color provided the Shaker interior with an accent that was never discordant or jarring. These subtle wood stains are equally appealing and useful in today's rooms.

Fabric

Collectors prize Shaker fabrics and textiles as much as their furniture. We can hardly wonder at this when we see these marvelously subtle designs.

Pick a Print

With a print like "Country Daisy," you have the choice of a small accent of color or a deep saturation merely by using the pattern in its positive or negative form. The negative version, midnight blue background with white flecks, is the number one best seller. People apparently love to live in a deep blue room offset by white trim and accents.

VISUAL TEXTURES

Raymond: "Country Daisy" is Gear's most loved pattern. With its simple motif of a fleur de lis or a cat's paw, it puts a small color accent on the wall. I think of it not as a pattern but as a visual texture. The design actually happened by accident. Originally, the flower had a little stem. But as the first samples came off the machine, the stem had been dropped by mistake. I knew instinctively that it made the design even stronger. Make the design process your friend. Take advantage of new discoveries as they happen. You, too, can gain something more exciting than you planned.

Add a Geometric

"Wainscoting" is a paper derived from the old wainscot panelling popular in the 1900's.

Mix a Floral

"Calico" is an overall tiny floral pattern with a soft movement to it.

Paint a Picture

"Appleyard" is the most pictorial wallpaper pattern of all. It's the complete opposite of the quiet visual texture of "Country Daisy" or "Calico" because it becomes a wall mural. Care has to be taken with how it's used so that it doesn't overpower the room with pattern. But people love it for its whimsy from another era.

David Riley

195

WORK WITH BLUE

Blue-and-white is one of the world's favorite color combinations. We find it in the designs of many cultures through the ages. But blue tones also mix harmoniously with other colors, especially with natural elements. The intensity of the blue will influence the room's mood. A desire for drama might lead into the deeper end of the blue spectrum, such as navy tones of rich, regal blue. The darker the color, the deeper the drama. Curiously,

Build on Blue

Gear's best-selling pattern, "Country Daisy," is updated in a new color, sky blue. Imperial Wallcoverings renamed it "Spring Daisy." How lovely the new color blends with yellow-ware bowls and country accents.

many people respond to these color-saturated shades. Wallpapers with a deep blue background are the best selling of all colors.

Lighter blues, on the other hand, result in rooms that are brighter and fresher in feeling. Blues tinged with red move into the purple family of tones, such as lilac and mauve. These are lovely in places where soft color is soothing, like the bedroom.

Mixing patterns is a growing trend. And there is a simple formula for combining them successfully, as you can see in these details. As you select patterns,

Mix a Floral and Stripe

"Hope Chest" is a fresh, blue-and-white floral that works amicably with "Wainscoting," Gear's narrow stripe by Imperial. Ironstone plates and strainers add crisp white accents.

TOM McCAVERA

CHARLES NESBIT

choose one of three basic types. They are a geometric, such as a plaid or stripe, a small-scale repeat, like that of a polka dot or a small floral that looks like one, and a larger-scale floral. These should all be related in color.

Color provides underlying unity that blends the patterns together. These detail photographs illustrate how to create small tableaux of your room scheme. Once your patterns are set, try them out with other elements that you intend to use in the finished room, such as white ironstone, country items, and weathered wood.

Use Blue and Barnwood

Weathered woods introduce soft wood tones to a country pantry. Old blue wood stain shows the rich patina that only age can give.

Try Several Plaids

Fabrics on throw pillows mix three plaids in different scales. A small one, "Homespun," is also the wallpaper. It is seen here with a grid, "Cats Cradle," and an even larger plaid. A fringed throw by Three Weavers brings in a subtle blue stripe.

LILO RAYMOND

DAVID RILEY

Blue-and-white star-patterned quilt, c. 1870, adds country charm.

Pine settee from Sweden was hand-carved during the Rococo Revival, c. 1790. It came from White Horse Antiques, Quogue, New York.

Wallpaper is Gear's "Apple Blossom," from Garden Graphics by Imperial.

Reverse the Color

Gear's "Blossom" print in periwinkle and white is from the Country Graphics group by Cohama Riverdale.

Tie It

Raymond: I like to tie on things, like these little quilted pads tied onto the backs of the settee and chair. It's a detail that's informal and friendly, and reminds me of the ties on a cook's apron.

CHANGE MOODS

The same print in tones of periwinkle blue and white gives two different moods simply by the type of furniture on which it is used. On the Scandinavian settee, left, the print expresses a sophisticated, updated country feeling—an unexpected choice for this elegant piece. Used on a little kitchen chair, below, the mood is rustic and relaxed for a casual dining area. The same fabric, used in different rooms, gives the house color unity.

Oversized tin tray is a
beautiful way to
serve the breads.

Gear's cotton chenille rug makes a blue placemat under bread tray.

Tom McCavera

CHANGE FROM PINK TO BLUE

Raymond: At Christmas time, we naturally redecorate the house for the holidays but there's no reason why we can't make quick changes to our home during the rest of the year. We arrived one Friday night at my beach house with our weekend guests and an array of brown breads for an easy supper of cheese, fruit, and wine. When we laid out the foods, there was a wonderful mix of colors: crusty brown breads, the purple-blue of the grapes. I thought it would be fun to pull out my blue-striped pillow slipcovers and switch the room's accents from the usual pink to a blue theme. It changed the whole feeling of the room and was a new experience for our old friends to see the room in a different color.

Change the Color Accent

We set out the breads on an oversized tray to play up the shapes and color of the crusty loaves. I bought a tin tray, one of four, at a crafts fair in Garrison, New York, for $15 the set and I use it constantly. Oversized dishes and trays make everything look spectacular. Then, to emphasize the blue color theme, I used one of Gear's cotton chenille throw rugs under the bread tray as an overscale placemat. The table was a visual treat of golds and browns massed together.

Make a Table

Everyone smiles at my coffee table made out of four goose decoys. I bought the geese at Pheasant Antiques in Bridgehampton, N.Y., and laid the glass slab across their backs.

NO-FUSS CHEESE MEAL

Maxime de la Falaise, food author: Who wants to cook when you're tired and hungry after a long drive to your house in the country? We were Raymond and Nancy's guests for the weekend. And we knew in advance what would be welcome for Friday night supper. Our house present was this delicious cheese spread, made the night before in anticipation of an informal evening of breads, cheese, fresh fruit, Normandy butter, and good red wine. This is the perfect meal for a casual evening of pillows on the floor, good conversation, and music. It was a no-fuss, relaxed evening for everyone.

Ring a White Platter

Raymond: To look at the crunchy cheese spread, sprinkled with berries and nut slivers, is to see it presented on a big ironstone platter, surrounded by whole nuts, grapes, apples, lemons, and berries. The round cheese is beautifully framed by the oval platter.

Cheese-on-Cheese Recipe

Serves 12–14
1 10" springform pan
wax paper, buttered
1 cup olive oil
1 lb sliced almonds
1/2 cup herbes de Provence
1 lb ricotta cheese
1/2 lb sour cream
1 packet gelatin
juice 2 lemons
1 lb brie cheese
2 bunches seedless grapes
1 lb goat cheese
1 lb blue cheese
4 pears
1 lb fontina cheese
1/2 lb crème fraiche

Butter pan.
Line bottom with buttered wax paper.
Sauté herbs, almonds in oil until golden brown.
Salt lightly, drain.
Mix together ricotta, sour cream, 2/3 of nuts.
Melt gelatin in lemon juice over heat until dissolved; add to ricotta mix; blend.
Remove rind of brie.
Cut cheese into long slices, arrange in concentric circles on bottom of pan.
Add thin layer of ricotta mix, layer of grapes, layer of goat cheese, thin layer ricotta mix, layer thinly sliced, unpeeled pears, layer blue cheese, thin layer ricotta mix, layer grapes, layer fontina as for brie.
Cover with wax paper. Refrigerate overnight. Remove springform and reverse onto serving platter. Peel off pan base and wax paper. Sprinkle with nuts. Garnish platter with grapes, fruit, nuts. Serve with a bowl of crème fraiche.

Tom McCavera

202

Grapes, apples, and nuts ring the cheese spread in a colorful necklace of blues, purples, and cream tones.

DRESSING A DOOR

Special occasions are the perfect time to dress up the house. At holiday times, especially, a joyful spirit suffuses the entire house and familiar rooms take on a festive air. We want the rooms, filled with family and guests, to express our happiness. Christmas, Thanksgiving, birthdays, weddings—all are reasons to rejoice.

The conventional way to decorate for important times is, of course, with flowers. Use flowers in unexpected

Gather the Greens

The first step in making a garland is gathering the materials: You'll need lots of one variety for the base. From the fields in Haverhill, New Hampshire, Amy chose armfuls of goldenrod and ironweed. For accent, she picked red zinnias from the garden. When you collect your own flowers, remember that the base flowers must have long stems. You'll also need a spool of florists' wire or picture-frame wire.

Fasten them Together

Begin by looping the wire around a handful of goldenrod stems. Do not cut the wire. Continue to lap more flowers on top of the first ones in regular intervals. Use the flower heads as your guide. Lap them so that the flowers you're adding lie just beneath the heads of those already fastened with wire. Keep twining the wire around the flower stems only, so that the wire forms a lengthening spiral around the stems as you progress. Lay the lengthening garland flat on the ground because it's easier to work that way. When the garland is the right length, cut the wire. Now the garland can be studded with zinnias and other flowers.

RAYMOND WAITES

RAYMOND WAITES

arrangements and places. There are many more ways to work with flowers than simply placing them in a vase. Wreaths, garlands and spectacular centerpieces are remarkably easy to make. All it entails is a fertile imagination—and armfuls of plant materials. Because flowers are expensive when you purchase them at a florist, look around you to see what nature has to offer. Fields and meadows abound in flowers. At most times of the year, something is blooming bountifully. Goldenrod, black-eyed Susans, Queen Anne's lace, chicory, field daisies, purple loosestrife, lupine, and beautiful grasses grow like weeds in summer and fall. Autumn also brings branches of colorful leaves, such as scarlet sugar maple, yellow poplar, rust oak, and vivid red sumac. Winter, while less verdant, provides fir boughs, holly, pine cones, pyracantha and other bright berries. In the South, nothing is more magnificent than the huge, glossy leaves of the magnolia tree. Use them all. Just how easy it is to make a garland from native greens is shown here, where Amy Wrapp assembled one for a bright blue door. It took about two hours to complete.

Hang the Garland

The completed garland was fastened to the doorframe with nails at each top corner and in the center. Wire was threaded through the garland and looped around the nailheads. A colorful garland makes a doorway a joyous sight.

LATTICE INTERIORS

S tanley Tigerman and Margaret McCurry Tigerman, architects: People are surprised when they enter the house because it looks like a farm building on the outside (shown opposite) but inside it's very well detailed. We don't think of the interiors as being highly mannered but as Shaker-like in their simplicity. Most of the millwork came from the lumberyard and the railings are plumbing pipes and elbows. The latticework of the sofa relates to the lattice exterior. People either love it or hate it. If they don't like the house, they're just very quiet and don't say anything at all.

Think Multi-Use

Both of us have children by previous marriages so the lofts have an L-shaped area with extra beds in addition to the work areas. For our parents we have another guest bedroom downstairs.

Half-round moldings are standard lumberyard millwork.

The loft is entered through an arched gateway.

Floors are white, vinyl asbestos tiles.

Howard Ka

Stepped soffit lowers the cathedral ceiling.

Save for the Future

I bought the fireplace mantel years ago in Nova Scotia and it's been in storage ever since. There's a native fisherman art on the island that is very appealing. When we built the house, the mantel worked nicely.

Relate Inside to Out

The interiors continue the idea of an agricultural building, like a barn, with a large central space and lofts on either side. Each loft, reached by the stair-ladders, holds a drafting table: Margaret's on one side and mine on the other. We both do a lot of work here on weekends.

Soften Modern with Folk Art

Margaret admires American antiques and folk art. Although she is a registered architect, she does primarily interiors, and she chose the windmill, all the decoys, the follies, and the Amish quilts. She is always poking around looking for things.

Research Your House

The house's original owner, Peter Wentz, was a second generation American whose father came from the German Palatinate. But no one really knows how the room's remarkable pattern originated or who painted it.

Make a Coverlet

Elizabeth Gamon, the museum director's wife, made the needlepoint coverlet in an 18th-century flamestitch when they couldn't find an old one for the daybed.

Copy the Design

The room's unusual pattern below the chair rail is easy to duplicate. Paint the wall flat white: mark off diagonal stripes and edge with dark paint. Add a final squiggle of the brush in the diamond's center.

208

This fine Philadelphia Chippendale chair may have come from Savery's workshop.

Michael Skott

Color a Treasure

Such a handsome corner cupboard is unexpected in a farmhouse. The carpentry suggests that the house's builders were familiar with the manor houses of the period.

Daybed comes from Chester County, Pa., but is not original to the house.

HISTORIC BLUE

Norma: George Washington actually slept in this charming bedroom in the Peter Wentz farmstead. The house, now a museum, was his headquarters during the Pennsylvania campaign of the Revolutionary War in 1777. So respectful of the room were the house's original owners that it wasn't painted except for one time in 185 years!

Restore a Fireplace

The room's fireplace had been removed. The museum's restorers put it back as close as possible to what it would have been. The paneling is very fine, typical of the grand houses in Philadelphia, 35 miles away.

A Traditional Style

Fishermen once made bed canopies in their spare time, using the same techniques they used to make fish nets. Netted canopies are beautiful, and modern versions can be purchased today.

An American Art

Quiltmaking was a way for frugal pioneer women to use fabric scraps. They traded pieces of gingham and cotton from cast-off clothes to gain the right colors and textures. Thus developed the intricate and original designs of traditional American quilts. Beautiful quilts like this one are still being made from old patterns.

Unity with Color

Color pulls this room together. The blue of the wallpaper is reiterated on the chair rail and wood trim to give the room a "finished" appearance.

FISHNET CANOPY

Canopy beds were originally draped, and developed out of the need to keep in heat and dispel drafts in damp stone castles. Trapping heat was still a factor in early New England homes. In the South, though, bed curtains were more effective for keeping out insects. Today, with improved windows and screens, bed canopies are purely decorative. But the magical memory of the early draped bed lingers on, and canopy beds have an irresistible appeal.

211

DAFFODILS
COPPER KETTLES

Yellow lemons, green limes, buttercups with green stems, honeybees, golden eggs. Yellow is a happy color that has many personalities. Sometimes it's as pale as the sand and wheat fields; other times it's brassy as a new penny. All of the sunny tones from daffodils to brass are warming influences in spaces. When you want to up the sunlight in a dark room, paint it yellow. In fact, rooms that face north and feel cold regardless of the weather will take on the temperature of a southern exposure. Paint the kitchen ceiling yellow and it is almost as effective at bringing in the sun as installing a skylight. In nature, yellow often comes paired with green. That's probably why this combination turns up so often in rooms, too. But the duo works best when one or the other is toned down. Bright yellow and bright green are too much competition for a single interior space. Whether you specifically choose yellow as the color base of your design scheme or not, you can't help using it. Yellow tones are present in many natural things, such as stripped pine and other wood grains, as well as in metals like copper and brass. Keep that in mind. <u>Norma</u>: Certain rooms seem to naturally want to be "yellow." Yellow always reminds me of the sitting rooms in grand old 18th-century country manor houses in England and Ireland—large, gracious spaces with high ceilings and moldings painted white. Yellow rooms look lovely with chintz fabrics and antiques, especially those in the darker woods. They probably used so much yellow in the British Isles because the weather is so changeable. Rain and overcast days are never very far away. Yellow rooms compensate. They're like rooms full of sunlight.

YELLOW AND GREEN

Raymond Waites

SHAKER YELLOW

The Shakers used utilitarian objects to enliven their rooms. These simple, elegant items give the Shaker interior an overall sense of calm and order. Yet while understatement is the keynote, these rooms are by no means dull. They are indeed examples of the vibrancy that can come from simplicity.

Hang Pegs

The practical Shakers hung nearly everything on pegs attached to boards on the walls. The pegs varied in length: narrow objects were hung on short pegs, but wider ones, like this kettle, were hung on longer pegs.

Color Can Accent

Shaker rooms are pared down to essentials in color as well as shapes, taking their interest from the juxtaposition of the tones of clay pottery, copper kettles, tin utensils, and wood. Yet the Shakers knew the value of using bright color on occasion. Here, a bucket sports bright yellow paint. A dash of color adds spark to a room of subtle tones.

216

ilo Raymond

Think Simple

When objects are similar in shape and compatible in color, group them together and store them on open shelves to make a striking display.

Work in Daily Objects

Daily chores were performed in a spirit of cooperation. We can imagine how the simple act of churning butter became a shared activity.

217

NATURE'S BOUNTY

Even the most casual supper for family or close friends can be festive. Arrange the setting around the preparation and presentation of the meal and have everyone join in the chopping and garnishing of the foods at table. Take the vegetables out of their paper bags and put them into pretty bowls. Condiments, too, and even the kitchen utensils should be part of your arrangement. Make a simple meal an occasion.

Vary the Shapes

Vary the shape and color of the bowls for foods and condiments to create a still-life composition that takes the place of a centerpiece. Fresh ingredients look especially appetizing when served in good-looking pottery.

Set for the Season

Coordinate your table setting with the season. In wintry weather, surround the dinner plates with fir branches instead of placemats.

Use Candlelight

Decant the wine into a colorful crock to let it air and to enhance its bouquet. Use candles at evening meals to shed a soft, romantic light.

Look to Nature

A yellow barn in the white snow exemplifies the beauty to be found in nature's colors every season.

YELLOW STRIPE

Yellow, freshened with white, is one of nature's beautiful color harmonies. The farmer's bowl, below, is the first piece of old crockery I ever collected. I loved its soft yellow and three wide white stripes. I measured the actual width and proportion of the stripe and translated it in the Gear fabric. This is an example of how we can be inspired by things from our past.

VEGETABLES, FRUITS, NUTS

Maxime de la Falaise, food author: We are returning to simple foods, each element cooked to its own perfection. The natural riches of the earth, its treasure of vegetables, fruits, and nuts, contain all the subtle flavors, proteins, vitamins, and minerals that we will ever need. A young carrot, a new potato, an exotic mushroom, an apple—all deserve as much culinary devotion as a rib steak or a brook trout. These glorious vegetable dishes, bursting with goodness and color, were inspired by what we found shopping at the farmer's stall on an autumn day.

Tom McCavera

Nutty Carrots and Onions Recipe

Choose shiny young carrots, small enough not to need slicing. Buy a basket of the tiny white pearl onions that are no larger than a child's marble. Get some hazelnuts, they will be almost as large as the onions! Use lots of finely chopped parsley—any fresh herbs, even mint, will be delicious. Chop some of the feathery carrot tops and mix in.

Boil the onions, without peeling them, in water just to cover with a pinch of salt and a scrap of bay leaf. Drain when tender. When they are cool enough, slip the onions out of their papery outer skin.

Steam the carrots very lightly with the nuts, lightly salted.

Toss the carrots, onions, and hazelnuts together with some walnut oil; season as needed, adding a pinch of dried thyme. Scatter the minced herbs on top of the vegetables and toss.

Brussel Sprout Tree Recipe

These whole branches of brussel sprouts can be found at country farmers markets and also in the city.

Clean off all the twigs and old leaves between each sprout and remove from each sprout any dead or yellowing leaves.

Lightly paint the sprouts with salted cooking oil. Place on a rack in a steamer, adding a pinch of baking soda to improve the color. Steam until the sprouts are tender to the point of a knife.

Lift out carefully and place on a folded napkin or on a serving platter. Guests can spear off the sprouts. Provide melted butter and a mixture of warm breadcrumbs and grated cheese in separate bowls for dipping.

Be Imaginative

Raymond: Serve vegetables so that their own beauty shines through. This brussel sprout tree is wonderful to look at all by itself. It made me think of a long narrow tray or platter to present it and I turned to a wicker basket-top for the server. The grid pattern in Gear's kitchen towel, folded long and narrow, complements the round sprouts. Once again, it's playing a grid pattern against a floral.

220

Yellow carrots and white onions look enticing in a big wooden bowl.

Fresh herbs add a flicker of green to carrots and onions.

Wicker tray and horn-handled knife provide additional texture and color harmony to the array of vegetables.

Be Inventive

The canopy is an old tablecloth that was in Tommy's family. It's all hand-drawn lace, and what a wonderful canopy it makes!

Challenge Yourself

This is Tommy's version of a pencil post bed. It's made of English oak. It took him about six months to find the wood and about two weeks to build the bed.

Lilo Raymond

LOOKING FOR GOOD BUYS

Tommy Simpson, woodworker, and Missy Stevens, weaver: When people say they paid $10 for this or that, you forget that they are probably looking all the time and may have bought something years ago. We go to a lot of shows and are always on the lookout for good buys. Most of what we buy are scraps that we make into things. The Irish chain quilt on the bed was only a pieced top and we made it into a comforter. It's tied, not quilted. When I find tattered old quilts, I'll make them into little pillows, like the cows on the bench. It's just a fun thing to do.

Find A Bargain

We call the quilt "Cookie Cutter Snowstorm." It's made out of grain sacks from the early 1900's. It looks like the person who made it heard about patchwork quilts but had never seen one. We bought it in New Jersey for $35 about four years ago.

Display Your Lovables

Tommy collected teddy bears long before it was the thing to do. One little bear wears eyeglasses just like Tommy's. (And he actually looks a lot like the little bear.)

223

Paint Brightly

The front door is painted bright orange to contrast with the apple-green trim. Note the humorous touch of the light bulb over the door.

Accent the Details

All of the room's details sport a different color. The molding creates a purple line at the chair rail.

224

Try it Unframed

Paintings don't always need a frame. This one looks best without one.

Howard Kaplan

COUNTRY COLOR

Sometimes it pays to use colors as bright as the rainbow. That's what Tom and Kirsten Beeby did in their weekend home, a converted schoolhouse in Wisconsin. Because the 1890's building, with its lighthearted charm, was itself so playful, the Beebys painted all of the architectural details a different—and shocking—color, adding their own playful touch.

Look for Local Buys

The Beebys enjoy hunting for regional antiques in the local Wisconsin shops. Their searches turned up both the four-poster bed and the patchwork quilt, which repeats all the colors in the room.

Stencil a Window

Kirsten Beeby designed the stencil for the window and painted it herself. It's a riot of color.

HOWARD KAPLAN

225

TREE SHUTTERS

When design isn't taken too seriously wonderfully creative rooms result. Chicago architect Tom Beeby and his wife, Kirsten, went looking for a weekend place, and they found a one-room schoolhouse sitting in the cornfields near Beloit, Wisconsin. (It is shown on the last page of this book.) Dating from the 1890s, the schoolhouse had at one time been used

Cut Out a Shutter

The windows were long gone so the couple replaced them. They also added the shutters with cutouts shaped like pine trees.

Shop Around

The Beebys found most of the furniture in local antique and used-furniture shops. Some are fine regional antiques; the rest are "making do." Small benches, for example, function as either seats or pull-up tables, and they sport shocking colors, adding to the house's down-home charm.

ard Kaplan

as a barn and was in disrepair. Parts of the wainscoted walls had been eaten away by weather, and the roof had a hole in it. The couple bought new wainscoting, which is still sold in some lumberyards, and completely restored the building, converting it for weekend use. Because all of the living takes place in the former schoolroom, the Beebys *couldn't* take design too seriously. They painted the interiors in many colors—apple-green below the chair rail, purple dado trim, and bright orange doors. "We wanted the joy of a summer day inside," the architect said.

Color the Trim

The apple-green of the trim is a color taken from nature, but it shocks in this colorful context.

Lay Down a Rug

An old woven rug, mellowed through years of use, puts a subtle strip on the pine floors.

227

Try squares for a
checkerboard face.

Put a teddy bear atop
a pumpkin.

Serve the kids a
sandwich house on
a wooden tray sur-
rounded by toy
animals.

This pumpkin is struck with stars.

Polka dots animate this jack o'lantern.

Hearts flicker with candle glow.

HAVE FUN
Next Hallow
set up a cen
piece of toy
jack o'lante
carved in fu
patterns. Ki

BLEND TWO PERSONALITIES

Raymond: Nancy bought this Majolica plate for $12. I wasn't wild about it because green isn't one of my favorite colors. I kept putting it away in a cupboard but, soon, it would migrate out again. Nancy obviously liked the plate and somehow it was always out on view. While looking for a birthday gift for her, I stumbled onto another collection of Majolica plates. These were sandy beige in color with touches of green leaves. I knew Nancy would love them so I bought the set of six for $30 each. When I saw them in the antique shop I thought about the table I would set with them and also the menu to complement the colors. Little pumpkin cakes, shaped like hearts, are just one small idea.

Pumpkin Cakes Recipe

2 8" baking pans,
wax or baking-pan paper
¹/₂ cup shortening
1 cup brown sugar
¹/₂ cup granulated sugar
1 egg or 2 egg yolks
³/₄ cup cooked, drained
mashed pumpkin
2 cups flour
¹/₄ tsp soda
3 tsp baking powder
1 tsp salt
²/₃ cup chopped nut
meats
¹/₃ cup sour milk

Preheat oven to 350°. Line bottoms of baking pans with wax or baking-pan paper; oil paper.
Cream shortening and sugar together; add eggs and pumpkin.
Sift together flour, soda, baking powder, salt, and cinnamon; add nut meats.

Add dry mixture alternately with sour milk to creamed mixture. Blend well.
Turn into baking pans. Bake for 25 minutes. Turn out and cool on racks.
With cookie cutters cut into heart shapes. Garnish with icing mix tinted yellow with food coloring and spiced with cinnamon.

Bake Cookies

Maxime de la Falaise, food author: The simplest cookies are often the best—especially when they are baked at home, scenting the house with whiffs of warm yeast, spices, hot sugar, and herbs. The presentation of simple food is as much an art as Japanese gift-wraps: pick the right colored dish for different cookies, add the personal touch of spring blossoms, autumn berries, and nuts.

Don't Match

Raymond: I've always collected flatware unmatched but related in style: handles of horn, mother-of-pearl, wood, or vermeil, embellished with similar motifs: flowers, animals, ancient monograms, bamboo, or shells. I mix them all together and every table setting is a fresh surprise.

230

Here are my favorite horn-handled forks.

Tom McClavera

Bittersweet stolen from the forest make a bright garnish.

STUFF A PEPPER

Maxime de la Falaise, food author: We love the familiar foods we grew up with: hot dogs, pizza, tuna salad, pasta, egg salad, chili, and apple pie. Try a new twist on these old favorites: put the hot dog between slices of fresh French bread, make pizza with a paper-thin crust, add fennel to the tuna, vodka to the pasta, saffron to the apple pie. This egg salad is different and delicious and it looks great stuffed in a yellow pepper. It's part of the harvest meal we created that works as well for Thanksgiving as it does for any day. For another variation, try stuffing the pepper with spicy chili.

Egg & Bacon Salad Recipe

Per pepper:
3 tbs heavy cream
5 eggs
3 oz butter
pepper, salt
1 cup mayonnaise
a pinch of favorite herbs:
basil, thyme, or tarragon
10 strips lean bacon
1 yellow or red sweet
pepper

Cut the "lid" off the top of the pepper, including the stalk. Scoop out the seeds and the white pithy ribs from inside the pepper. To a bowl add the cream and break the eggs into the cream.

Add half the butter in small pieces, the salt, pepper, and herbs. Whip up with a fork until foamy.

Melt the remaining butter in a skillet, add the egg mixture and scramble lightly. Remove pan from heat while eggs are still quite runny and continue stirring until they cool and set. When cold, mix with the mayonnaise, adjust seasoning, and fill the pepper.

Fry bacon until very crisp and dry. Drain well. Garnish eggs and pepper with bacon strips. Serve with crackers or toast.

Color Your Table

Raymond: This is a simple and delicious dish, but the presentation makes it spectacular. To frame the bright yellow peppers, we put them on a small terracotta plate inset into a larger patterned one. (You saw the same plates on page 163.) This created a wreath around the peppers. It needed a final garnish, so a sprig of bittersweet from the back yard was laid across the plate.

Ornate plate frames the peppers.

A bittersweet twig adds garnish.

Tom McCavera

Brighten with Color Accents

Raymond: There was something wonderfully relaxed about this quick pasta supper. The bright red and yellow pepper rings around the bowl suggested the yellow accents of round pot holders used as placemats and the casual placement of wooden serving tools. A wooden box holds the cutlery and napkins, acting as an informal centerpiece. The box is part of Gear's "Wood Blocks" collection by Maleck. We served icy beer at this meal instead of wine. You'll note that we even dared to put the bottle on the table. Who says it shouldn't be done!

Wire and wood scoop serves the meal.

A squeeze of lemon is a must on pasta.

Tom McCavera

234

Final crack of fresh pepper is delicious on pasta.

Gear's round pot holders make colorful pla... mats.

Cold Pesto Pasta Recipe

4 servings
½ lb green pasta shells
½ lb white pasta shells
Cut into julienne strips:
4 small carrots
1 zucchini
8 broccoli flowerettes
12 green beans
1 whole chicken breast, poached, skin and bones removed
pepper, salt
a few tbs olive oil
2 cups mayonnaise
1 cup pesto sauce (fresh or bottled)
½ cup pine nuts or crushed walnuts
2 yellow or red peppers
1 bunch fresh basil, parsley, or dill, minced
4 garlic cloves, minced
In boiling, salted water, cook the pasta until al dente. Drain, rinse with cold water, put into a mixing bowl, toss with 2 tbs oil, salt, pepper.
Steam the vegetables a few minutes; they must be al dente.
Pull chicken meat apart with fingers into rough pieces: 1″ x ½″.
Toss pasta, vegetables, and chicken together. Season.
If bottled mayonnaise is used, stir in 1 tbs olive oil. Mix mayonnaise, pesto sauce, nuts and fold into pasta. Pile the pasta with sauce into a serving bowl. Slice peppers into thin rings; arrange around rim of bowl. Sprinkle pasta with herbs and garlic.

RED PESTO PASTA

Maxime: Pasta may have originated elsewhere, but it's become a naturalized American meal. Cold pasta dishes are part of our nouvelle cuisine and for good reason. They're quick, nearly foolproof, and open to all kinds of innovation with a change of ingredients. All that's needed is a light, oil-based sauce to bind the elements together. The sauce should cling to each piece of pasta — penne, rigatone, the ridged surfaces of macaroni, the corkscrew shapes of fusilli, and the larger shells are designed to cradle the sauce. On a cold day a cold pasta dish can be heated in the oven and served piping hot. Hot or cold it's delicious.

FALL LEAVES SET THE THEME

Raymond: I remember from my childhood those old steel engravings that show the Pilgrim families at their first Thanksgiving. They are grouped around a harvest table enjoying the fruits of their first harvest outdoors. Whether they actually ate outdoors or not, it's still a great way for us to savor the last of Indian summer. It's only a little extra effort to set up the table under the trees, put on light sweaters, and celebrate fall foliage. The colorful leaves set the theme for the table: the green leaves of the Majolica plates, the golden bowls and crockery, and for a centerpiece, an ironstone bowl brimming with russet, scarlet, orange, and purple leaves studded with bright red berries.

Dine Amidst Nature

We set up the table in a leafy glade—the warm wood tones looked lovely framed in greenery and speckled with sunlight. This was the setting for our harvest meal of pilgrim's pie, brussel sprout tree, nutty carrots, and pumpkin pie. The country pottery and rustic cutlery all echoed the autumn tones and leafy theme, creating a feast for the eyes as well as for hearty appetites. As the sun set, the candlelight took over, flickering from the pumpkins carved into jack o'lanterns.

Green Majolica plate continues the leafy motif.

Bowl frames the autumn colors and looks beautiful on a pine table.

Find New Uses

Raymond: Throughout all the table settings, you see the same things used in different ways. Here are Nancy's heirloom chocolate service, coin-silver spoons, and her heirloom pickle forks, which we use throughout the meal from hors d'oeuvres to dessert.

Spike the Brew

All sorts of flavors enhance a cup of coffee: rum, cognac, bourbon, white crème de menthe, Tia Maria, vanilla, nutmeg, cinnamon, lemon, orange. It's fun to group these flavors on a table, in bottles and small bowls, and let each guest pick a favorite. A big bowl of whipped cream is always popular, for these flavors can be added to the cream, rather than to the coffee itself.

238

Gilt curtain tie-back is put on the table for visual pleasure. It has no other use but to delight the eye.

Serving with golden bone china makes the dark coffee look especially rich.

Lemon adds color and a squeeze of extra flavor.

COFFEE DELIGHTS

Maxime de la Falaise, food author: Buy coffee in the bean and grind it yourself. It stays fresh much longer. My mother, who adored full rich coffee, used to spread the day's supply of beans in an even layer on a baking tin, sprinkle brown sugar over the top, and bake the beans in a low oven until the sugar melted over them. This gave a delicious nutty flavor to the brew. Coffee imparts a wonderful flavor to all sorts of chocolate desserts. The very finest grind can be sprinkled over the tops of cakes, mousses, and ice cream as a tasty garnish.

Hobo Coffee Recipe

Grind a heaping tablespoon of coffee for each cup and warm it in a saucepan over low heat; sprinkle with sugar. Boil as many cups of water as coffee needed plus one for each 6 cups. Throw coffee into the water, lower heat, cook it, stirring, for 5 minutes. Rinse out cheesecloth in hot water, place it, double-layered, on the top of a pre-warmed coffee pot; pour the coffee from the pan through the cloth into the pot. A real hobo would keep the coffee grounds and re-use them. We don't suggest you do!

Use Your Best

Nancy Waites: These cups and saucers are part of a chocolate service that belonged to my great aunt. I don't think they were ever used. Raymond and I make up for it, though, by using them all the time. There's a little flower at the bottom of each cup which you see after you've finished drinking.

239

Round pot holders act as little trivets for the cups.

Bunch the Daisies

Formal arrangements are lovely but they can take too much time to create. Simple arrangements are easier and quicker. Buy (or pick) a big bunch of flowers, clip the stems, and toss them in a big container. They'll look terrific.

Fill a Basket

While visiting Ben and Bonnie Helms, I bought a large bagful of squash at the farmer's market. When I got it home and put it in a big basket—it looked skimpy. To make the squash look more dramatic, I crumpled up the brown paper bag and used this as filler material underneath the squash. I even like the brown color showing through.

240

CENTERPIECES

Raymond: There are so many natural things around us that we don't use to advantage: field grasses, wild flowers, bright berries, vines, colorful vegetables such as squash, lemons, apples, oranges. They make handsome centerpieces and are as beautiful as a floral arrangement. I like to build little stories around natural elements and my country objects such as my duck decoy nesting in a pine box. Use the country objects you collect every day. Don't treat your treasures as too precious to touch. Bring them into your daily life and build your own tableaux around them.

TOM McCAVERA

COPPER STORAGE

Barry O'Rourke/Stock Market

**TALLIC
CENTS**

uster of cop-
pots sends
rkling reflec-
s through
country
hen. Don't
lerestimate
power of
tallic accents
reative color
emes.

BLACKBOARDS
PEWTER

Scotty dogs, caviar, pearls, ravens, limousines, tuxedos, penguins, blacksmiths. Black is the most dynamic of colors. It spells sophistication, luxury, enchantment. Black is also strength and boldness, as expressed in wrought-iron hardware. It's also historic. Many country Windsor chairs were stained black. Pewter gray was a color used on moldings in 18th-century American homes, such as the Peter Wentz farmstead and Sue Bruckner's 1812 house, both shown in this chapter. The House of Seven Gables, in Salem, Mass., is stained a deep pewter gray. Black also suggests candlelit dinners, New Year's Eve, moonlit nights. Black and dark gray are often the choice for certain city environments. Many people with hectic careers see their living spaces mostly at night. Then, these rooms come alive with company and dramatic lighting, like a diamond glittering on a basic black dress. Gray is black softened with white. It, too, is sophisticated but soothing and calming. Gray is a particularly good choice for tailored, refined rooms. It is the new neutral of the 1980's, mixing with naturals, such as sand-beige. Raymond: It was a major decision to wallpaper my city loft in black and gray tones. I had been living with white and naturals. As you will see in this chapter, black became the foil for my country collections and red accents. Be warned, though, because black shows every bit of dust and soaks up most of the room's natural light. But nothing could be more spectacular at night.

SARAH HARTMAN

SPECIAL MOMENTS

Visual Moments

Raymond: Life is a mosaic of small moments, of visual treats experienced in a second, like the silhouette of this pitcher against a patterned wall. They are also moments that involve all of the senses— taste, touch, smell, sound. As you plan a dinner party, think about the fragrance of fresh flowers, the warm touch of wood, the crisp feel of linen, the coolness of glass or marble, the elegant smoothness of silk. A house pulls all of these special experiences together. This is the way we bring beauty into our daily lives. You may not be able to do an entire home but you can start with one of these single moments and build on it. Linked together, such special moments add up to a total life experience.

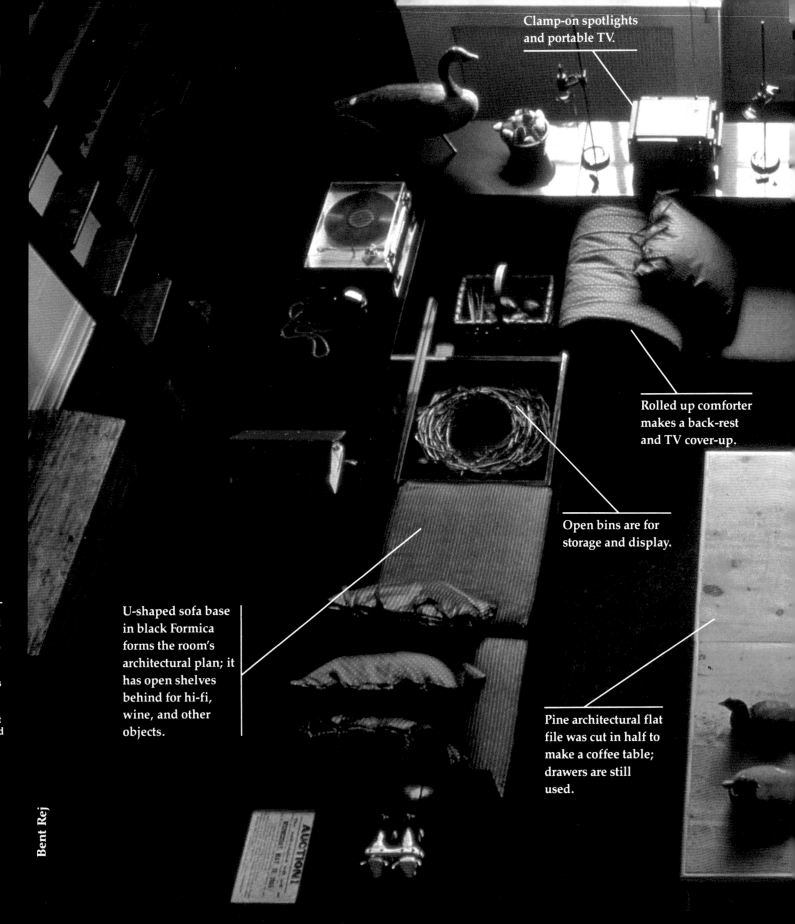

Clamp-on spotlights and portable TV.

Rolled up comforter makes a back-rest and TV cover-up.

Open bins are for storage and display.

U-shaped sofa base in black Formica forms the room's architectural plan; it has open shelves behind for hi-fi, wine, and other objects.

Pine architectural flat file was cut in half to make a coffee table; drawers are still used.

ON'T
GHT IT
aymond: I love
bjects—old and
ew. I don't buy
em, they jump
ut and buy me!
always fight
y guilt feelings
bout buying
ne more won-
erful thing. But
y life is flooded
ith things, my
iends. Every
w months, it
ems too clut-
red and I hide
l my friends in
pboards. But,
owly, they all
me out to play
ain.

Bent Rej

Platform countertops wrap around the seating, displaying collectibles.

Sit and sleep units are made from pillows by Butterick Patterns.

Oversized bowl masses red flowers.

Duck decoys started the room's color scheme.

Mix Styles and Periods

I like to see old mixed with new. Designs from different time periods work wonderfully together. Here, it's a high-tech lamp from Conran's, the portable TV, and all my country pieces.

Dress a Sofa

Here is a basic formula for mixing prints: the stripe, on the pillow against a simple dot. Pillow cover with tab ties is a Butterick pattern no. 6048, which you can make.

Roll up a Comforter

Comforter in Gear's "Firefly" print is rolled up as a pillow and doubles as a cover when guests sleep over. I also curl up in it when I lounge in front of the TV.

250

Use Antique Boxes Today

Antique pine chest that used to store herbs now organizes small items and magazines.

NESTING INSTINCT

Raymond: My home is my nest. I like to surround myself with the objects that speak to me, like my quilts, little pine boxes, and decoys. Everything in the room is black, gray, and pine with red accents—my favorite colors. To me, spaces must be adaptable and relaxed. Since I'm a lounger, not a sitter, the seating in my loft is just upholstered pillows with comforters rolled up as back-rests. The room has to work for Nancy and me when we're relaxing at home as well as when we bring in a crowd of friends.

Think Dual Function

Nancy and I don't have a formal guest room and sometimes we put up weekend guests on the sofa.

Raised platforms are surfaced in Formica's grid pattern. They wrap around the sofa cushions for sleeping or lounging. Backs are open storage shelves.

251

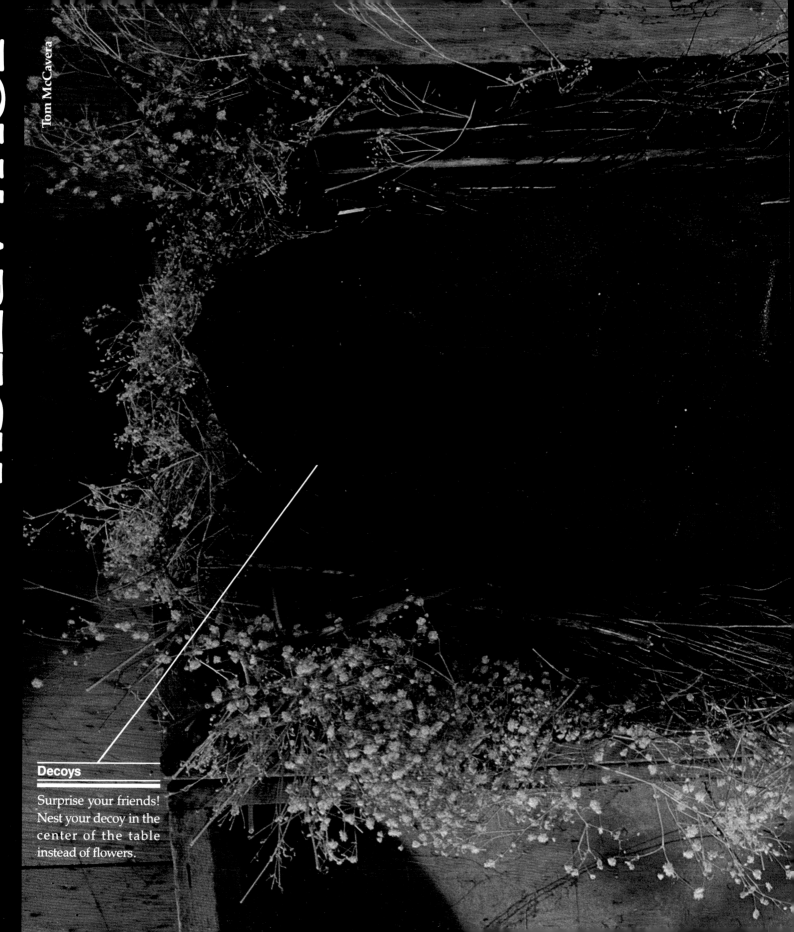

FOLK ARTECH

Tom McCavera

Decoys

Surprise your friends!
Nest your decoy in the
center of the table
instead of flowers.

Line with Silver

A small silver bread plate is used as a liner for the Tiffany plate. The porcelain bowl in a double-handed server layers china on silver. The plum soup was a calculated choice, adding a rich color of its own.

Create a Focus

The simple grid pattern of the tablecloth acts as a frame against which to play off the symmetrical arrangement of dishes and serving pieces.

Mix Materials

The fine Tiffany plate is set on a round, black plastic tray, used as a placemat. The plate cost $200 and the oversized tray cost $8. It's all right to mix expensive and inexpensive items.

Shed the Light

The modern lamp highlights the table setting, shedding light on the table's center. Its sleek design offers a contrast to the antique silver and flatware.

Arrange Symmetrically

Coffee service and cups are set in a line with the antique silver dome, creating a visual anchor for the eye. Other silver objects radiate around it.

A LIFETIME OF TABLE TREASURES

Raymond: Our table setting repeats the loft's colors—black, white, and red. We have used color to edit our tableware collection. The key element was the silver that Nancy inherited from her great aunt and great-grandmother. Although we tend to entertain casually in the country, we keep the silver in the city so our table here ends up quite sophisticated. Over the years, we have been buying a certain plate pattern. When we first got married in 1968, I gave Nancy her first plate. It's Tiffany's "Black Shoulders," and it sold then for $75 each. Every Christmas, I would buy her another plate. At first, we could only serve two people on this service, Nancy and me. Today, we have a set of twelve plates and they now sell for $200 each. It took us a lifetime to build the porcelain set but it was something that we both really wanted and it was well worth the wait.

ROBERT GRANT

Hang a Dollhouse

Antique dollhouse hangs on the wall like sculpture. It repeats the soft grey tones of the wallpaper, "Polka Dot," from City Dimensionals by Imperial.

Start a Collection

Dollhouse, the first one I ever collected, was the start of my collection. I found the architectural simplicity appealing. It's very much like the houses in the front section of this book—direct and functional.

Build Storage

Wooden drying rack is fitted beneath the counters to store wine glasses, china.

Use Baskets

Baskets are great for storing small, unrelated items. They keep things handy but hidden.

Bent Rej

256

Enlarge the Space

Lining one wall in mirrors doubles the sense of space, reflects light back into the room, and enhances the effect of shuttered windows.

Adapt Antiques

Ironmonger's cabinet is ideal for storing things for the table—silver, cutlery, table linens, and napkins—in its little drawers.

INSTANT CHANGE

Nancy Waites: Our dining room in the city is small and the kitchen is tiny but that doesn't stop us from entertaining. We found an old blacksmith's cabinet that we've put to double use. The little tool drawers are great for storing our silverware, cutlery, and napkins. We made a new top for the cabinet with a piano hinge that opens up into a dining table. We use the top for preparing the food and then open it up for entertaining. The mirrored wall gives the room the illusion of greater space.

BENT REJ

BENT REJ

257

Make Do

Wallpaper in the early colonies was imported and expensive. People had to make do with imaginative decorative effects for walls, such as stenciling and sponge painting.

Spot a Wall

You can duplicate this engaging pattern by painting your walls flat white and then using a brush or round sponge to dot on the pattern. When your friends ask about the fun wall design, you can tell them it's a historic pattern from the Peter Wentz Museum!

Michael Skott

Mantlepiece holds a selection of local Pennsylvania redware.

Fan-back windsor was probably made in New England.

HISTORIC SURPRISE

Norma: When the Peter Wentz farmhouse in Worcester, Pa., was being turned into a public museum, the house's restorers were surprised by the colors and patterns they found on the walls under the old paint. As the layers were scraped off, out emerged a riot of chocolate-brown polka dots. It would seem that even our Colonial ancestors enjoyed bold, graphic designs on occasion. Enough of the original patterned walls remained to prove that these remarkable designs actually dated from the mid-1700's.

Echo the Pattern

The polka dots in the summer kitchen are glimpsed again in the winter kitchen on the other side of the breezeway. This gives the eye a delightful pattern play.

Built-in wall cupboards are common in stone farmhouses of the time.

Ladderback chair is typical of eastern Pennsylvania.

Dutch cupboard of pine came from Bucks County.

MICHAEL SKOTT

CHECKERBOARD BARN

Ken Le Van, industrial designer, Carole Le Van, weaver: When we bought our stone farmhouse in Pennsylvania, it came with this big barn. The barn was a raw space with nothing in it. In fact, one half, a later addition, was caving in so we tore that off and restored the barn to its original size. We turned one section of the barn into our studio for Carole's looms and my drafting table and woodworking shop. We did the farmhouse in Pennsylvania Farmhouse Colonial but our barn is somewhere between American and French Country. It's quaint and rustic but there's also a computer in here. We both love checkerboard so we installed a big black-and-white checkerboard tile floor in the studio.

Stash the Yarns

I made the bin for Carole's yarns. She is a textile designer as well as a weaver and does most of her designing here in the barn studio.

Make Your Table

Ken: The table looks old because I made the legs from old barn timbers, which I turned on a lathe to look like those on an old farmhouse table. (I puttied in the cracks.) The top is made from sycamore planks. The table is nearly nine feet long and took about a week to make.

PEWTER GRAY

S ue Bruckner, antiques dealer: I'm a nut about finding and rescuing old things. When my husband and I left New York to get away from commuting, we bought this 1812 house in Haverhill, N.H. I'd poke around and drag home damaged things or furniture that needed work. I'm not bad with a hammer and saw and do a lot of refinishing. Soon the house was full and I was still dragging things home. A friend said I should open a shop. I had a lawn sale. I was that crazy junk lady, but dealers soon took me seriously—they taught me more than books ever could. I always buy what I like. I find things for a little because I can see under the millions of coats of paint.

Paint Them to Match

The chairs are all different. I bought them one at a time and painted them all the same red color to match.

Buy it in Pieces

The table was in pieces, but I could tell it was a Pennsylvania hutch table without a top. I offered the owner $200 for the base and she thought I was nuts. All it needed was a major glue job. When a friend redid the kitchen in her 1790's house, she gave me two beautiful old left-over pine boards and that became the top.

Colonial lamps are rare. This candlebox would sell for about $300.

Spindle chairs cost about $40 each.

Lilo Raymond

262

Pine mantle board was a freebee from the local lumberyard.

Settle bench, an old potty chair, cost $70 way back when I bought it.

Build a Set

I paid $12 for my first pewter plate and it was full of holes. My kids teased me about buying an old garbage can cover. I plugged the holes with liquid steel and still have it. Each year, I'd buy another pewter plate. The room's colors came from my old pewter.

Hook Your Rug

I hooked the rug over many winters when my kids were small and I was bored with childrearing. It's made of wool skirts, wool coats, wool anything. Every winter, I'd add another foot.

Open shelves show off a duck collection.

Glass doors bring in view and breezes.

Shell hiding a light bulb is an ingenious lamp.

Stair banister is a display rack for quilts.

Join the Fun

Bonnie: We spend a large part of our weekends cooking, entertaining—and eating. The kitchen is under the skylight, in the center of the house. Everything is out in the open so we can be with our guests and participate in the activity while preparing the food.

Pick a Color

Raymond: Ben and I love the color of sun-bleached driftwood and we wanted to bring it into house design. We developed a stain for Gear's "Wood Blocks," a collection of wood products made by Maleck, Ben's company. The pickled pine floors and all the cabinets are in this subtle tone.

Fridge sits in its own alcove.

Rag rugs keep sand from being tracked through the house.

Tom McCavera

WEEKEND REFUGE

Ben and Bonnie Helms, Gear manufacturers of wood products: Bonnie and I work sixty hours a week. Our beach house is our refuge—we can't wait to get here on weekends. Looking for folk art and other elements for the house is our hobby, and color influences all our purchases. It's a marvelous way of editing things. When we see something we know immediately whether it will work or not. We want an aesthetic continuity, no confusion or visual pollution to disrupt the eye.

Keep it Open

Raymond: When we began to plan this room, we wanted a neutral background of sand-beige color. Everything that is brought into the space, influences its mood: quilts, baskets, flowers, even foods. Each season as the local foods and flowers change, the house changes its color accent. One day, the accent can come from the yellow of squash, the next day, it might come from the red of tomatoes.

265

Open counters show
what's cooking.

Wood grid for hang-
ing pots and baskets
will become scattered
with objects.

Painting rests on the
floor and can be
moved around.

Stairwell beneath the
skylight is in the
house's center.

Platforms with
shelves behind form
bases for the sofa.

Windows inside link the spaces by day but provide privacy at night.

Black is the accent color used throughout.

Tom McCavera

Raymond:
Blown-glass candle-
stick, from Pheasant
Antiques, East
Hampton: $60.

Dolphin-shaped
candlestick, from the
Metropolitan Muse-
um's reproduction
collection: $48.

Crystal candlestick,
picked up in the
south of France:
$150.

Art Deco pressed-
glass candlestick,
from a Brooklyn
antique shop: $15.

Tiffany candlestick
of faceted glass:
$200.

Thrift shop find: $2.

Crystal wine
decanter: Nancy's
grandmother's.

Charles Nesbit

CRYSTAL GLITTER

Natural

Blue

BERRY
BRIGHTS
The primary
colors of the
rainbow are
echoed in na-
ture's harvest—
berry reds and
blues, yellow-
green pears, and
bright oranges.

Red

Orange

Yellow green

Show Your Colors

America is the land of independent spirit. This one-room schoolhouse is dwarfed by the Wisconsin cornfields—but inside it's a cornucopia of color, which you saw on page 224. America's colors, patterns, and forms are free for the taking. Use them. That's what we mean by living home.

AMERICA.

NASA

A

American Artech, 6–9, 134
Antiques, selection of, 102–103
Appliances, energy-efficient, 104

B

Barns, 12–13, 18–19, 49, 51, 260–261; Gear Barn, 64–65, 104–107; new, 156–157; red, 71; yellow, 20–21
Barwick, Jo Ann, 189
Baskets, 168–169, 178, 240–241, 256
Beams, 53, 64, 177
Beds, 88–93, 183; canopied, 150–151, 210–211, 222–223; four-poster, 224–225; pencil post, 222–223
Beeby, Kirsten and Tom, 224–227
Black, 245, 250–251; as accent, 267; and pink, 136–137; and red, 252–253
Blue, 189–199, 210–211; shutters, 39; window frame, 47
Brooks, Marge, 79
Bruckner, Sue, 80–81, 262–263

C

Candles, 61, 69, 107, 168–169, 218–219, 268–269
Centerpieces, 241
Chairs, 160–161, 165, 176–177; antique, 102–103, 208
Christmas decorations, 104–108, 204–205
Church, clapboard, 32–33
City loft, 248–251
Climate, style influenced by, 49–50
Collections, 248–249; barn animals, 148–149; bears, 223; by color, 162–163, 175; crockery, 174–175; display of, 84–85, 160, 264–265; dog paintings, 98–99; dollhouses, 256–257; kitchen tools, 80–81; silver, 76–77; tools, 78–79; toys, 94–95, 119
Colonial architecture: church, 32–33; windows, 50
Color, 166; autumn tones, 20–21, 112–113, 236,

270–271; change of, 201–202; collecting by, 163, 175; and design, 8, 56–57, 62, 66–67; seashore, 160; *See also* Black, Blue, Gray, Green, Naturals, Pink, Red, Rose, White, Yellow
Comforters, 90–91, 146–147, 250
Cow feeders, 105, 139
Crystal, 268–269

D–E

Davis, Hal, 98–99
Dayton, Robert, 11
de la Falaise, Maxime, 108, 118
Design: color in, 66–67; components of, 8–9, 56–57; process of, 60–63; scale in, 98–99
Display techniques, 84–85, 94–95, 128–131, 160, 264–265
Doorways, 38–43, 177, 224
Energy-efficient design, 34–35, 64–65, 104
Entertaining: 165, 180–181, 218–219; birthday party, 142–143; for children, 118; theme parties, 108–109

F

Fabrics, 65–67, 197, 250; design ideas from, 56–57
Factory, converted to shop, 171
Fireplaces, 178–179
Flatware, 76–77, 110, 164; unmatched, 230
Flower arrangements, 164, 240
Folk art, 166–169, 207; houses, 116–117
Food colors, 105, 137, 180–181, 220–221, 270–271
Fox, George, 32
Furniture: antique, 258–259, 262–263; handmade, 176–177, 180, 198–199, 260–261; mixed styles, 160–161, 165; pine, 124–125, 129; Shaker, 158–159, 192–193; wicker, 126–131

G

Gamon, Elizabeth, 208
Garlands, 204–205
Gear Barn, 64–65, 106–107; kitchen of, 104–105

Gold, Charles, 170
Gray, 245, 250–251, 262–263; and pink, 136–137
Green, and yellow, 213–215
Greenberg, Michael, 94–95, 175, 184–185
Greenhouse, in barn, 64–65, 106–107

H

Helms, Ben and Bonnie, 160–161, 181, 240, 264–265
Home Sweet Home, 10–11
Houses: adobe, 22–23, 46, 48, 50, 53, 121, 178–179; azalea, 14–15; beach, 180–181, 264–267; folk art, 116–117; historical, 28–29, 208–209, 258–259; lattice, 30–31; modern, 34–37; pink, 121; Pueblo, 24–25, 39; saltbox, 10–11; stone, 26–29; yellow, 16–17

I–J–K

Idea sources, 56–57
Industrial art, windmill fragment, 18
Jacobsen, Hugh Newell, 34
Kitchen tools, 80–81
Kivas, 178–179

L

Ladders, for display, 85, 128–131
Lattice house, 30–31; interior, 206–207
Lee, Mother Ann, 159
Le Van, Carole and Ken, 26–27, 260–261
Lighting, 168–169, 264; clamp-lamp, 252; doorway, 38; spot lights, 180; *See also* Candles

M

Magazine clippings, 60, 62
Metallic colors, 163, 213, 242–243
Mirror walls, 256–257
Mood, development of, 57, 61–63, 68–69
Mortar, restoration of, 26–27
Musham, Bettye Martin and Bill, 58–59, 64

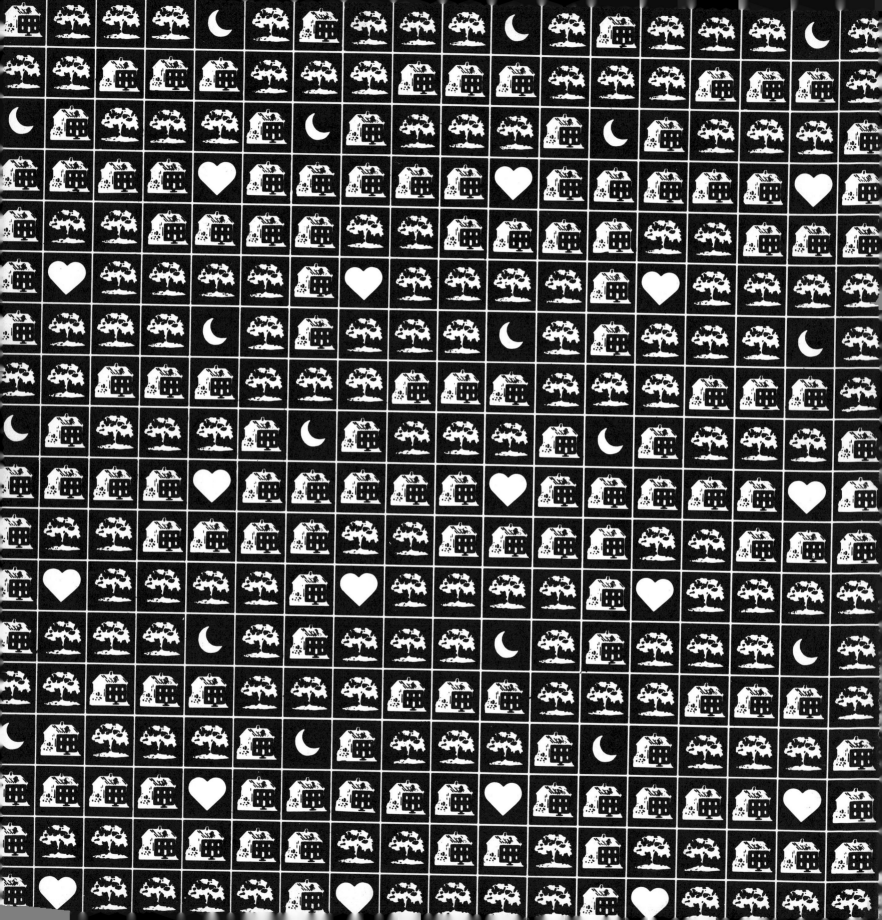